Thinking Thing[s]

General Editors
Graham Slater and C. S. Rodd

3. The Christian and People of Other Faiths

Thinking Things Through

Thinking Things Through

3. The Christian and People of Other Faiths

Peter D. Bishop

EPWORTH PRESS

ISBN 0-7162-0514-9

First published 1997
by Epworth Press
20 Ivatt Way,
Peterborough
PE3 7PG

Typeset by C. S. Rodd
Printed and bound by
Biddles Ltd
Guildford and King's Lynn

Contents

General Introduction

The great German theologian, Hans Küng, has said that his aim in all his writings is to enable his readers to hold their faith with confidence and not with a bad conscience. This new series, prompted by the conviction that Christians need to think through their faith but often lack appropriate help in so doing, has a similar aim. Moreover, the assistance that it seeks to offer is related to another conviction: that many church members need persuading that theologians are concerned in any way with their problems and that theology can be at all relevant to their lives.

In such a situation, it is essential, we are sure, to begin with life and with church life. Only in that way can we be confident that we are dealing with grassroots issues. Plainly, however, it is not enough to identify the questions where they arise; we must also indicate the sources of help – if not of all the answers – in as non-technical a way as possible.

In some volumes, these tasks will be tackled in sequence; in others, they will be interwoven. Whatever the precise format, however, our hope is that, through this interaction, difficulties will be faced, fears dispelled, open discussion promoted, and faith informed and strengthened.

The books can either be read by individuals on their own or used in groups. We hope the questions at the end of each chapter will be useful both as a check that the text has been understood and as a spur to reflection and discussion.

Later volumes will deal with such issues as the problem of evil and suffering, the sacraments, life after death, Jesus, the Holy Spirit, creation, salvation and discipleship, prayer, making moral decisions, science and religion, and presenting the gospel.

GRAHAM SLATER AND C. S. RODD

Introduction

How Christians relate to people of other faiths is of great and increasing importance. What once might have been regarded as a rather 'academic' subject is now a pressing concern for Christians in Britain. Many have neighbours who are Hindus, Sikhs, Muslims, Buddhists or Jews. Children from Christian homes will go to schools that are multi-faith in their composition, and will be introduced to aspects of some other faiths in their religious education as well as by being part of multi-faith school communities. Even those who live in areas of the UK which have remained monocultural will encounter issues in education, public policy and above all in religious belief and practice which require some thought about how the Christian is to relate to people of other faiths.

This small book is an attempt to help people to think through these things. Part 1 is in the form of case studies in which we meet people who, although fictional characters, are all set in situations based upon experience and upon long and careful study of Britain's religiously plural society. The case studies focus upon meetings of people, for dialogue can only be between people. The reader is invited to share in the dilemmas and discussions that arise out of such experiences as that of parents being faced with their daughter's marriage to a person of another faith, or of a church responding to an invitation to host an inter-faith celebration.

Part 2 then examines some of the thinking behind inter-faith issues in a slightly more theoretical, but I hope still very accessible, way. There is cross-referencing between the two parts, both by indicating in brackets the chapter and page in which similar issues are discussed – e.g. (chapter 1, p. 1) – and by adding to questions in Part 1 references to questions on the same general area in Part 2. It is hoped that in using Part 1

vii

groups will reflect widely on what for them arises out of the case studies, especially in relation to their own experiences - so only two questions are suggested for each chapter.

Part 3 contains brief accounts of the major faith communities in Britain today, telling how they became established in the UK, providing outlines of some of their beliefs, and indicating the kinds of religious practices in which they engage.

The reference numbers refer to the Notes which appear on pp.112–114.

I am grateful to Graham Slater and Cyril Rodd for encouraging me to contribute a book on this subject to the series, and for their helpful comments on an earlier draft, and to Sarah Ball for her help with the typescript.

PETER D. BISHOP
APRIL 1997

Part 1

Inter-Faith Experiences

1

The Inter-Faith Celebration

The local inter-faith group seemed a lively affair. Robert, the newly-appointed minister of a city-centre church, had been invited to join the executive committee, and had arrived for his first meeting. Getting to the meeting had not been easy. As a newcomer to the city he was already aware of how long it could take him to find his way from the manse in a comfortably suburban area to the other side of the city where the cheaper housing was mostly located. Driving in the dark with a map on the seat beside him, he recalled the now alarmingly frequent experience of planning the route carefully beforehand only to miss the vital turning or to be ambushed by a surprise one-way system. It was on these narrow streets that some of the younger members of his generally prosperous congregation lived. The houses would not be described by estate agents as 'starter homes' but that was their function for young upwardly-mobile Central Church members. It also appeared to be the area where most of the other faith groups in the city had their headquarters. Three mosques, two Sikh gurdwaras, a Hindu temple, three different kinds of Buddhist centres, and the Progressive Jewish synagogue were all located within a couple of miles of each other among the gloomy streets in this poorer part of the city. Was there something symbolic, he wondered, about the inaccessibility of other faiths for the comfortable Christians on the 'right' side of town?

If the streets were gloomy, the company was not. A friendly group of people, some in the traditional dress of their cultural or faith communities, had gathered in a large room in the partly reconstructed building which served as a temple, or gurdwara, for one of the Sikh communities. Coffee and various kinds of sweets had been served. There seemed to be no lack of volunteers to provide refreshments. Showing hospitality to visitors, whatever their faith, was clearly important, and the

3

pleasure the hosts took in that was evident. Apparently it was this group that had been hosts the year before to a city-wide inter-faith celebration. The main item on the agenda that evening was the next celebration, planned for One World Week in October.

Robert had been warmly welcomed. As the meeting progressed he became aware of attention focussing on him as people wondered aloud where this year's inter-faith celebration might be held. They had been to gurdwara and Hindu temple, to mosque and synagogue, but not yet to a Christian church. Indeed, they had had some difficulty in getting a Christian minister on to the committee. Robert felt his first twitch of alarm. Was he to be regarded as the representative of all the Christians in the city? With the alarm was a rueful amusement at the thought of how some Christian communities would react to the idea of his being their representative. But more to the point, what would his congregation, after only a brief acquaintance, think if he were to offer the spacious premises of Central Church as the venue for the inter-faith celebration?

The hospitality and friendliness were beguiling. He could hardly suggest they tried some other church, unrepresented among the committee. The Quakers were the likeliest, of course, but were their premises large enough? No, he would have to offer his own place. The committee members were delighted, and proceeded to discuss the content of the celebration: the theme would be peace; there would be readings from the scriptures of various faith-groups; several groups would provide appropriate music; and in response to a quiet Buddhist intervention, it was agreed that there should be time for silent reflection. Robert made his way home. The first thing to do was to ensure there would no clash of dates and bookings, although with two to three hundred people expected they would have to meet in the church itself. Then he must try to rally support. How embarrassing it would be if those hospitable

4

people came to Central and found only a handful of his church members present!

The Elders and the Church Meeting agreed to the proposal that the inter-faith celebration should be held as planned. But Robert felt that there was an underlying unease among some of the members, and perhaps even more worrying, a widespread view that this was a somewhat odd thing to do, but that if he wanted to get on and do it, that was his business. The morning after the Church Meeting he had a telephone call from Rebecca, a young steward, lay preacher and pastoral visitor who did an enormous amount of work for the church and was involved in almost everything that went on. Robert had noticed that she had been uncharacteristically quiet during discussions about the celebration. Now she wanted to come and talk to him about it.

Robert did his special hospitality bit, offering a cup of good filter coffee and biscuits, and trying to set Rebecca at ease. It wasn't easy. Rebecca had had a distinct conversion experience five years before; her conversion and Christian commitment meant the world to her, and she had assumed as a matter of course that her clear and particular beliefs represented a set of final Christian truths which should never be compromised. Should the church not be organizing meetings that might convert people to Christian faith, rather than helping to display the values of other faiths? There seemed to be an inconsistency between what she took to be the primary mission of the church and the proposed inter-faith celebration. Perhaps those who felt as she did should not be expected to be involved in such an activity.

Robert and Rebecca talked for a long time. The first thing Robert wanted to say was about hospitality. He had learned at the inter-faith committee that when previous celebrations had been held the host community had been very strongly represented. Even at the committee meeting he had sensed the pleasure taken in providing hospitality to visitors. That was evidently an important part of both the cultural and religious backgrounds of the other faith groups. As he spoke, Robert felt the onset of a kind of panic. What would those kindly people – Sikhs, Hindus, Muslims, Jews – think if they came to Central Church and hardly anyone from the local church community was there to welcome them? Was it conceivable that the principles of good natured people like Rebecca could inhibit their natural tendency to be hospitable? A little grudgingly, perhaps, Rebecca took the point.

Robert went on to explain that what was intended was an inter-faith *celebration*. There was no intention of somehow coercing people to worship in ways that were unacceptable to them, or indeed to worship at all. There would be readings, from scriptures and perhaps other writings in the various traditions; there would be music and songs; there would be moments of silence; but the meeting would deliberately exclude the faith-statements which say or imply, 'my religion is better than yours'. People would be invited to hear, appreciate and reflect upon what the faiths had to say about peace. They would not be put into the situation of compromising their own beliefs, unless – an unlikely event – their beliefs were *opposed* to peace. The challenge of the meeting, which he hoped would be a strong one, would arise from the theme, and so might lead to thoughts such as those expressed by Hans Küng: '. . . there can be no world peace without religious peace'.

Related to that, said Robert, was the contribution that religious groups made, for good or ill, to race and ethnic relations in the city. Most of the other faith groups (the exceptions being the Buddhist groups) were made up of people whose family origins lay in other parts of the world. That was obvious in the case of Muslim connections with Bangladesh and Pakistan, Hindu roots in Gujarat and East Africa, and Sikh ties to the Punjab. Even the apparently well-assimilated Jews had family memories of a migration into this country which had taken place over the past hundred years. A firm rejection of people of other faiths would be seen not only as a negative stereotyping of the religion but also of their cultural and ethnic backgrounds. Rebecca objected to that. Surely, one had a duty to proclaim the truth, and could not compromise because that might upset somebody? But she could see what Robert meant. Oh dear, this was more difficult than she had supposed. Perhaps there was a conflict between pursuing what seemed to be admirably Christian aims, like world peace and harmony between different races, and particular ways of expressing Christian doctrine.

Over a second cup of coffee they moved on to the heart of Rebecca's problem, which had to do with how the teaching of the Bible and the church could be consistent with a tolerance of other faiths. When she stuck to proof texts, such as the conclusion of Matthew's Gospel, she felt she was on to a winner. 'Go to all nations and make them my disciples; baptize them in the name of the Father and the Son and the Holy Spirit.' That was clear enough, surely? Robert was uneasy. How far should he go in discussing the current state of biblical criticism? He had always felt this to be a bit of a problem. On the one hand, a minister wants people to understand the Bible. But there are different ways of doing that. If he went too far in the direction of revealing what many scholars say about such a text, would he not be in danger of undermining Rebecca's obviously vibrant faith? He responded, rather lamely he later felt, by pointing out that Jesus had commended the faith of a Roman centurion and a Syro-Phoenician woman, without any evident expectation that they would change their religious faith or practices as a result.

The long meeting ended on a positive note. Robert and Rebecca felt that they understood one another better, and fully appreciated each other's motives even if they did not agree completely on ideas and beliefs. Rebecca was much happier with the planned inter-faith celebration. She could accept willingly that Central Church had a duty to be welcoming hosts to those who would attend the meeting. Anything less would be a denial of her own Christian faith. She appreciated that such a celebration would not require her to set aside her own beliefs, and might enable her to understand better the faith of other people. She also glimpsed something of the importance of encouraging better community relations, and began to think of this as a significant part of any church programme.

Questions for Discussion

1. Was Robert right to have been so concerned about hospitality? How would you have responded to the request from an inter-faith group?

2. To what extent, if at all, do you sympathize with Rebecca's problems about the inter-faith celebration?

See also questions 1, 2 and 3 on pp. 45, 46, and 3 on p. 82.

2

The Yoga Class

The property committee had a lot of experience of dealing with difficult problems. Even the apparently simple matters of deciding what colour to paint the toilets or whose responsibility it might be to clear up after the ladies' keep-fit class could consume hours of their time. The more controversial issues, such as whether to re-arrange furniture in the sanctuary, replace the pipe organ with an electronic instrument, or change the faded church carpet, were problems of a different magnitude altogether. By comparison, altering the creeds would be a simple matter. But here was an issue which some thought did have doctrinal significance.

There had been a request from a local teacher of yoga to rent the Methodist church hall once a week for her yoga classes. The property committee would have to come to a decision about the matter, and then pass its recommendation on to the church council, which would have the final say. The word 'yoga' appeared to cause some disquiet. Was this not a form of religious teaching? Mr Barnes wanted to know. His apparently limitless knowledge of CPD (*The Constitutional Practice and Discipline of the Methodist Church*) could often intimidate members of this and other committees. He thumbed through the copy he always carried with him to property committees, church councils and circuit meetings, and pointed out that Standing Order 920 requires the trustees to 'accept general responsibility for the teaching given at all . . . non-Methodist public religious meetings held on Methodist premises'. The possibilities for debate seemed endless. Yoga classes certainly sounded non-Methodist; but would they constitute 'religious meetings', and in any case should they be regarded as 'public'? Clearly one or two members of the committee who agreed with Mr Barnes regarded yoga as very definitely religious teaching, and of a kind which was incompatible with Methodist teaching.

9

They were not sure precisely what was involved, but supposed there might be some danger of brain-washing in such an activity. Mrs Wenham didn't agree with that, but she did have her own worry. Might such a class held on the premises give the impression that the church was actively encouraging faiths other than Christianity? And if people from the congregation began to attend, might that lead them eventually to seek, say, meditation classes at the local Buddhist centre?

Fortunately, one of the committee knew the young lady who ran the yoga classes, and was able to assure the members, to their relief, that she was not at all religious.

The first issue to be talked through was the worry that a yoga class might be some kind of 'cult' activity. It seemed to be the use of a word from a different cultural and religious background that gave rise to the suspicion that, whatever it was that would be taught, it must be something both inappropriate and unwholesome. Sheila, who had been minister of this church for the past three years, knew the people well enough to recognize that particular fear of the unknown. There were those – and they included some of the most loyal and hard-working members of the church – whose outlook was very much conditioned by the Methodist sub-culture in which they had been brought up. They were not of the generations who had mixed much more freely with people of many different outlooks, of other faiths and none, during their formative years. Their schooling had been too long ago to have included a broadly based religious studies element. They did not travel widely or read very much outside of their own immediate concerns. Even their choice of newspapers was such as to encourage rather than to challenge an insular view of people of other nations, languages and cultures – although church life and teaching inhibited the more hostile expressions of such attitudes often found in the media. Sheila tried to reassure them that whatever yoga was or was not, it certainly could not be

10

regarded as a 'cult', intent on luring people into some closed and secretive society.

Henry Jones was a new member on the property committee. He had showed a certain degree of impatience with some of the discussions that had taken place during his first two meetings, and had adopted a largely silent, almost surly pose. Now he became more animated. He was a teacher who, although not a specialist in religious education, knew something of what was taught in his school about religions. Only recently he had glanced through a syllabus in which the opportunity 'to participate in periods of stillness and quiet thought' was expressed as one of the key aims, and was linked to several lessons on yoga. Henry explained that the yoga taught in the kinds of classes they were now considering was almost always *hatha yoga*, that is, one part of a much wider yoga tradition which emphasizes posture, breathing, stillness and concentration. It is usually taught as a method of gentle exercise and as a means of quietening the mind and disciplining the body. Most people attending yoga classes of that kind, he felt, would not regard it as a religious activity at all. It was hardly likely, he argued, that this could be construed as the encouragement of religious faiths other than Christianity.

That rang a bell with Sheila, who recalled that although her ministerial training had not included the study of non-Christian religions, it had introduced her to an article on 'Christian Yoga'. The writer had claimed that 'The method of classical Hindu Yoga is a clear and helpful contribution to Christian devotion, and could provide many Western Christians with a much needed practical stimulus to the rediscovery of a spiritual discipline.' She had not been entirely sure about that at the time, but in the light of Henry's remarks suddenly saw a welcome opportunity to divert the committee from its proper attention to property matters and connect it instead with the church's worship. Mrs Wenham was worried about young people being so influenced by yoga classes on the premises that

11

they might go off to a Buddhist meditation class. But wouldn't it be wonderful if the presence of a yoga class were to encourage people to think about, say, moments of quiet in worship? Or the possibility of introducing some structured meditation into Sunday worship? They were all good at the noisy parts of worship; was there something they might learn about the use of quietness and stillness as a form of worship? Sheila was quite excited! Perhaps the introduction of this item at the Church Council could be a real opportunity to move people along rather than a difficult piece of business.

Encouraged by Sheila's comments, Henry took up the argument by saying how good it would be if the routine letting of the premises could encourage people to come on to the premises for an activity which had religious as well as secular roots. Although there was little doubt that most of those enrolling for a yoga class would see it as a form of exercise, it was possible that a few might want to make a connection between that and forms of worship which included meditation. It wasn't only young mothers who might be tempted from a secular meeting on the premises into the church's worship. If they followed up Sheila's suggestion perhaps one or two yoga *aficionados* might find their way into a service which included periods of stillness and quiet thought.

The idea seemed to generate enthusiasm among several members of the committee. It was good to see direct connections between their role as property people and the wider life of the church. It really would be something if, out of their discussions, there could emerge ideas about a little more silence in worship and, who knows, even the beginnings of a meditation class. This wasn't just keeping things going and maintaining the fabric. This was being creative. They agreed to recommend letting the premises to the yoga class. But they hoped for much more.

The Yoga Class

Questions for discussion

1. Did Mrs Wenham have a point? To what extent, if at all, do you share her concern?

2. Sheila was excited by the prospect of using the discussion of yoga to introduce some quietness and stillness into worship. From what you know of Christian congregations, what do you think their reactions would be?

See questions 1, 2 and 3 on p. 50.

3

What Happened to the Jews?

John found his working life increasingly difficult. Over the
previous three years more than twenty-five per cent of his
colleagues had been made redundant, and whilst for some that
had meant an early introduction to a pleasant and well-
resourced retirement, for others it seemed to mark an
unpleasant and premature end to permanent employment. There
were now less of them to do the work, but more work to do all
the time. He knew that this was a common experience. More
and more people knew they would never again have more than
short-term contract jobs, and those who hung on to regular full-
time work had to work harder and harder, with the implicit
threat that if they did not they too would join the ranks of the
short-termers or the unemployed. Inevitably, there were social
consequences of that. People at work were more tense, and had
less time to spend socializing with one another. Sadly, it
appeared that it was increasingly difficult to be pleasant to
people or to show interest in the lives they lived outside the
workplace.

John was a person who found considerable support in the life
of his local church. There was less time available these days to
attend meetings or serve on committees, but he did manage
most weeks to attend a Bible study group, and he rarely missed
worship on Sundays. It bothered him that many of the things
discussed in the study group, expressed in the music of
worship, and declared in the preaching were very difficult to
apply in the place where he spent most of his waking hours – at
work. His church made enthusiastic plans about evangelism.
The fact that the nineteen-nineties were declared to be the
decade of evangelism provided added impetus to suggestions
that evangelism should be at the heart of the church's
programme. From the pulpit there were frequent exhortations
to practise evangelism among the unchurched in the places
where they lived and worked. Church members had a
responsibility, it was said, to speak about their faith to their

neighbours and to those with whom they worked. That was the cutting edge of evangelism!

In principle, John agreed. But the temporary enthusiasm induced by a rousing sermon on a Sunday seemed to evaporate alarmingly quickly on a Monday morning. The principle might be right, but the practice of it was quite another thing. His colleagues were a mixed bunch, and one of the few things they appeared to have in common was a dislike of religion and the religious. If reference was ever made to religion he could be sure that it would be negative. It wasn't so much that his colleagues were indifferent to religion, as used to be the case and as his church appeared to assume; it was rather that they despised religion as a kind of institutionalized hypocrisy. There was one exception. If John felt close to anyone at work these days, it was to David. On the rare occasions he had mentioned anything about his own faith or religious practice to David, he had felt he was talking to someone who understood. Religion was important to David, too. But David was a Jew. He quite often attended synagogue on Saturday mornings, but even more important was the family meal together on Friday evening. David was a friendly and humorous man, good at his job but also easy to talk to. John was always very reluctant to say anything about his faith to his other colleagues; he was sure they would not understand what he might try to say. But with David that difficulty did not arise.

One Sunday morning when the sermon was again on the theme of evangelism, there was special mention of Christian evangelism among Jews. The preacher quoted with evident approval St Paul's words about his fellow Jews:

> For they ignore God's way of righteousness, and try to set up their own, and therefore they have not submitted themselves to God's righteousness (Rom 10.3).

There was no doubt, said the preacher, that Christians still have an obligation to try to convert Jews to Christian faith. He spoke eloquently about the heroic labours of Paul in trying to convert his compatriots to his new-found faith. Should we do less, he asked? The rhetorical question hung in the air as the sermon ended. It buzzed around inside John's head for the rest of the day. He would have to speak to David about this, but he was not at all sure how he could do that.

An opportunity arose the next week for John to have lunch with David. John had calmed down since Sunday, and the zeal he had felt then was tempered by discretion. He decided to approach David obliquely on the subject of the claims of the two religions. As a progressive Jew, David was used to discussion of issues which arise in Jewish-Christian conversations. Instead of responding directly to John's tentative question about how Jews regarded Christian evangelism, David spoke appreciatively about Jesus as a Jew. He quickly filled in some of the background to festivals that Jesus would have celebrated, and – it was news to John – suggested that when Jesus read from Isaiah in the synagogue at Nazareth it would not have been in the context of a synagogue 'service', but as part of the reading, expounding and discussion of scripture that occurred among groups of men whose acts of worship would have taken place in the temple.[1] David's lively and informed descriptions of Jewish practices as they might have applied to Jesus opened up a whole set of new ideas for John. Clearly, there were many things about the roots of their own faith that Christians could learn from Jews. Perhaps he had better exercise a little discretion about this business of evangelizing among Jews until he had looked into these matters more closely.

Two weeks later, John and his wife Mary enjoyed one of their rare weekends away. The friends they were visiting were people they had known for a very long time but saw only occasionally these days. It was a pleasant reunion. On a gentle Saturday afternoon walk John found himself walking with Ted, while Mary and Ted's wife, Jane, followed at some distance. Usually it was the women who had the more animated conversations. But once John introduced the subject of Jewish-Christian relations, his previously halting conversation with

Ted took flight. Ted, he learned, had for several years been a member of his local branch of the Council of Christians and Jews, and gradually had found his perceptions of Jews and Judaism altering. He was glad to hear about the conversation with David, for that confirmed his own experience of how an appreciation of Jewish life and practice today can illuminate some of the teaching of the Gospels. Ted had recently been reflecting upon the fact (for fact it undoubtedly is) that Judaism is much more interested in practice than theory, with doing the right things than with theology. His new Jewish friends suggested that this is why a reading of the Gospels shows Jesus saying very little that we would recognize as 'theological'; he was much more concerned with what to do in certain specific situations – typically Jewish. And what a strange feeling Ted had when he read the comment of a Jewish writer that 'Jesus never ate non-kosher food in his life'.[2] Getting to know Jews could be a very enriching experience for a Christian.

Ted then opened up some of the unpleasant parts of Jewish-Christian history. Until a visit to Israel led him to visit the Museum of the Diaspora in Tel Aviv it had not occurred to him how much persecution Jews had endured in *Christian* Europe. In ways that he had not yet worked out, there did seem to be a connection between certain kinds of Christian theology and anti-Jewish sentiments. Was it possible, he wondered, that conventional ways of reading parts of the New Testament could contribute to negative stereotypes of Jews? It was only recently that he had begun to wonder why the Gospels often referred to 'the Jews' as a community of people distinct from Jesus and his disciples. Were they not all Jews? The question had never occurred to John, and now that it had been raised he felt quite worried by it. Perhaps there were things for which Christians needed to make amends.

That led naturally to a discussion about evangelism. In meetings between Christians and Jews should the main purpose of Christians be to convert Jewish people to Christianity? Or was that simply a continuation in another form of the misrepresentation and misunderstanding that the two men were now beginning to be aware of? The New Testament, after all, had some harsh things to say about 'proselytizing'. According to Matthew, Jesus had said of some of his contemporaries: 'You travel over sea and land to win one convert; and when you have succeeded you make him twice as fit for hell as you are yourselves' (Matthew 23.15). Could such words, often used to strengthen the stereotyping of Jews, actually apply to the Christian who sought Jewish converts? It was a worrying thought. Perhaps there is a difference between an evangelism in which the Christian tries to share the treasures of his faith with other people, without applying pressure or uttering threats and certainly without denigrating the traditions of others, and the proselytizing which is simply the desire to increase the influence of one's own group. John was beginning to feel that his conversation with Ted was opening up thoughts about the relationship between Christians and Jews in ways which the sermon in church had not even begun to do.

It was a long walk, and they arrived back at the house as the warmth of the afternoon was beginning to give way to the chill of evening. A welcoming fire and tea awaited them. John and Ted had talked as they had rarely done in the past. John's conclusions, as he slumped gratefully into an easy chair, were that it might be more helpful to practise hospitality and increase understanding than to encourage people to move from one faith to another. Perhaps he should seek out his nearest branch of the Council of Christians and Jews, and discover what could come from meeting and knowing the people who still held to the faith into which Jesus had been born.

Questions for discussion

1. Do you agree with John's conclusion, following his discussion with David, that he 'had better exercise a little discretion about this business of evangelizing among Jews'?

2. How many of the things Ted had discovered about Judaism did you know? What things surprised you? In what ways have they altered your attitude to the Jews?

See Questions 1, 3 on p. 54, and 2, 3 on p. 68.

4

Christians and Muslims

It was a blustery day, with wind and rain scudding across the nearby hills, complementing the grey stone of the inner city houses, and emphasizing the dullness of the winter days. It was difficult now to remember these same streets as they had looked in the height of summer, windows and doors open, little plots of garden adorned with roses, the bright summer clothing of the residents, all acting as light to the shadows of the houses themselves. Penelope and Simon had recently moved from the more benign climate of the south to these sharper northern streets in pursuit of career opportunities and more affordable housing. They were the sort of people who read the Sunday supplements and garnered bits of information about a higher standard of living enjoyed by people in 'the north' who spent less of their income on housing and therefore had more of it available for the pleasures of life. Not that Simon and Penelope were mere hedonists. They both had firm and radical political views and supported campaigns to cancel third-world debt, ban nuclear weapons, and end racial prejudice. In their previous southern county town, it has to be said, their principles were more theoretical than practical. Here there were challenges on the doorstep that would test and refine their political ideas.

The area in which they had bought their pleasant three-bedroomed terraced house was largely occupied by Muslim families. In their part of town, the majority of Muslim families had their roots in Pakistan. Back in the nineteen-sixties the earliest Pakistani male immigrants had been joined by wives and families. Soon, within the space of a few streets, families that had lived in the same small towns of rural Pakistan reconstituted their communities, with Pakistani shops, restaurants, cinemas, travel agents, and banks. Penelope, who had studied social anthropology at college, was delighted to recognize these signs of what was technically called 'boundary maintenance'. The original newcomers were now in their sixties or seventies. Many of them lived with children and grandchildren in the houses that they themselves had bought back in the sixties.

Simon and Penelope were anxious to establish good relationships with their neighbours, but were not sure how best to go about that. Simon managed occasional conversations with Akram, the head of the family. Akram was a friendly man of about fifty. His elderly widowed mother lived with him, together with his wife Ayesha and their three children, who ranged in age from twenty to fourteen. At first Simon felt that their conversations were stilted. But when he asked about the children the response was much more promising. The younger two were still at school, and the parents' involvement with their children's progress and their worries about it were evident. Their elder daughter, Farida, had been to a single-sex girl's school, and was now at university. Her parents were very proud of her progress, and had high expectations of her. Changes in the local education system had meant that their son and younger daughter both attended the same coeducational school. Simon thought it interesting that although the family were obviously practising Muslims, they had preferred to send the two younger children to a Catholic school, where they felt the discipline – and the academic results – were better, and where there was the attraction of religion being taken seriously, even if it was the wrong religion. But clearly there were worries about the sixteen-year-old daughter, Alifa, being in a mixed school, and the kinds of social and peer group influences that she was likely to encounter there. In spite – or was it because? – of their own upbringing in Britain, Akram and Ayesha were very uneasy about the possibility of Alifa having a boy friend. Her social life, they felt, should still be within the family, among relatives, and within the Pakistani community.

As time went by and the conversations became easier, Simon and Penelope became increasingly aware that many of their

Pakistani Muslim neighbours did indeed have social lives which were almost entirely contained within their own community. Visiting relatives and friends who all came from the same area of eastern Pakistan and now all lived within the same few streets was the main social activity. On the rare occasions that they ate out, it was almost always in a Pakistani restaurant (why did people always call them 'Indian restaurants', Penelope wondered?). Akram and Ayesha were practising Muslims, and so attendance at mosque and Muslim fasts and festivals also played a significant part in their lives. Evidently, the children had all been through the time-consuming practice of attending Saturday morning Arabic classes at the mosque. For Muslims, it is important that their scriptures, the *Qur'an,* be read in Arabic. Penelope and Simon were amazed by that. From their own church background they knew how difficult it was to get children to attend Junior Church; but just imagine expecting them to learn Hebrew and Greek in order to read the Bible properly!

Gradually, the conversations became frank enough for real criticisms to appear. Simon and Penelope were surprised to be confronted with views of British society which they found troubling, even though they acknowledged the truth that lay behind them. Clearly, members of the Muslim communities felt that a society built upon Islamic values was greatly superior in terms of morality and social behaviour to Christian societies (and for them, reasonably enough, Britain was characterized as a 'Christian society'). That was especially so in the case of family and sexual behaviour. Simon and Penelope were a little surprised by the forceful way in which both Akram and Ayesha expressed the view that it was wrong for couples to live together before marriage, and thought they had better keep quiet about their own situation. The Muslim couple appeared to be astonished that Christian churches at least tacitly sanctioned such practices by conducting the weddings of people who had been living together for years. Clearly these practices were

22

related to the lack of parental control of their children, the casual way in which British children dated, and the alarming complacency of parents who allowed their daughters to go out unsupervised with young men whom the family did not know. All this seemed to be asking for trouble. When it was put like that, Simon and Penelope found it difficult to defend what did look like extremely casual methods of introducing young people to potential partners. They talked about the need of young men and women to meet a variety of people of the opposite sex before they could make proper decisions about marriage. But when their neighbours retorted by quoting recent figures for the divorce rate in Britain, that seemed a bit feeble.

The concern of Akram and Ayesha about family life in Britain also found expression in their surprise at the way in which many people seemed perfectly happy to consign their aged parents to old people's homes. They had heard stories of sons and daughters who had not visited their elderly parents for months or even years once the parent had been safely tucked up in a residential home. Where was their respect for the elderly? How could they treat older members of their own families in such ways? Penelope argued that many residential homes for the elderly were excellent places which could provide facilities far better and more appropriate than would be available to an elderly person left alone at home, or even living with a family in which everyone else went out to work. But she was aware of an uncomprehending disapproval.

It gradually dawned on Penelope and Simon that some of the things Akram and Ayesha said about British behaviour and social practices were drawn from the media, and especially from television. They had had no close British friends outside of their own community. As they watched British society through the window of their television screen, they saw a world in which sexual promiscuity was an accepted way of life for almost everyone (even, to their astonishment, for some celibate clergy). Television also confirmed the impression of Britain as

23

an extremely violent society. A lot of the drama they watched centred around the two themes of hospitals and the police. In both, violent assault, offensive language, and lack of respect for authority were commonplace. Nowhere did there appear to be the clear guidelines, rigorous punishments, and code of conduct based explicitly upon religion which was so evident back in their parents' home country of Pakistan. Surely, British society should be governed by Christian law in the way that many Islamic societies were governed by the teaching of the *Qur'an* and the law code of the *Shari'ah* ?

In the light of these early conversations, Simon and Penelope made a conscious effort to get to know their Muslim neighbours better. They made contact with their local inter-faith group, and through that with the Inter Faith Network for the United Kingdom. They attended meetings which included discussion of specific issues in Muslim-Christian relationships. They bought a copy of an English translation of the *Qur'an* and read some introductory books on Islam. Slowly, their discussions with Akram and Ayesha took on a clearer form, and they were able to address contentious issues. Gradually a new understanding dawned for all four of them. They came to appreciate ways in which the faiths of Islam and Christianity share so much: a common inheritance going all the way back to Abraham, and reflected in material found in both the *Qur'an* and the Bible; a common belief in revelation; and the fact that both are 'religions of the book'.

As their discussions continued, they were all able to acknowledge that Christians as well as Muslims have a concern for moral values and the need for higher ethical standards in public life. But they had to acknowledge that there are different ways of expressing such concerns. The expectation that a 'Christian law' should be more explicit in British life (an expectation shared by many British Christians) was seen to be based on a fallacy. It was only after a lot of thought on the subject that Simon and Penelope realized that the New

Testament is not a book of commandments or laws. In that sense, Christian values could not be expressed simply and directly in law, although of course they could inform and undergird the law. Perhaps that was why English law was based upon Roman law and not upon some imagined 'Christian law'. Jesus himself had taught by illustration and story, by teasing out the inner meanings in his own Jewish tradition, by inviting people to think about particular situations, rather than by laying down a rule for all time and all places.

That led on to the thought that a closer adherence to the Gospels might encourage greater tolerance of a variety of faiths in multi-cultural Britain. It connected with ways in which their thinking about race relations had been developing. They had been shocked to read in one study of British Muslims the calm assertion that: 'Britain does not have a tradition of religious or cultural tolerance of non-Christian outsiders.'[3] Clearly, it was necessary to accept the rights of believers of different kinds within an essentially secular framework. In doing that, they realized, Christians, Muslims, and members of other faiths would need to acknowledge that a common feature of all faiths is that their adherents find it easier to admire than to emulate the teachings set before them.

Questions for discussion

1. How do you react to the suggestion that 'Britain does not have a tradition of religious or cultural tolerance of non-Christian outsiders'? To what extent might Christian belief have contributed to this situation?

2. Simon and Penelope made a considerable effort to acquaint themselves with Islam in order to understand their Muslim neighbours better. Is there a lesson in that for us all?

See questions 1, 2, 3, p. 68.

5

'We all believe the same things, don't we?'

The community centre was humming with life. A group had
come in to use the sports hall, the toddlers' group was in
session, the Asian Women's group and the 'Back to Work'
group were meeting. This was also one of the mornings when
the main user of the building was a Christian charity which had
been set up to help parents and children in bed and breakfast
accommodation. Two or three mornings a week parents whose
circumstances had forced them into such circumscribed
surroundings were able to bring their children to the centre.
Play facilities were provided, and activities organized, for
children who otherwise were confined to one or two rooms,
where, apart from watching television, there was hardly
anything to do and a constant demand not to make a noise. It
was also possible for parents themselves to spend the morning
drawing, painting, or engaging in other activities more creative
than trying to keep the children quiet and drying the washing in
a single room. The clients who made use of these facilities
were varied. They included women who had been forced out of
their family home by the violence of their partners; teenage
mothers forced into bed and breakfast accommodation by
overcrowding in the family home; families who were refugees
from war-torn areas of Africa; and children from travellers'
sites where the prevalence of drugs and the brutality of police
trying to catch the dealers often left children uncared for in
windowless caravans set in an ocean of mud. The helpers at the
sessions were frequently amazed at the privation endured by
these families, and moved almost to tears by the vulnerability
of children with an enormous need for love and practical care.

Although the charity was a Christian foundation, drawing
helpers from a variety of churches in the city, the clients were
of all faiths and none. This sometimes led to discussions as to
whether, if at all, the faith of the helpers should be made

explicit in the running of the centre and in dealings with clients. Those from more evangelistic backgrounds tended to the view that Christian faith was one of the things on offer; others were of an opposite opinion, maintaining that any attempt to use the work of the centre for evangelistic purposes would be to compromise its integrity. For the latter group, the work itself was an expression of Christian faith; what anyone else made of it was their (or perhaps God's) business.

One of the regular problems the centre tried to deal with occurred when families were moved from bed and breakfast accommodation to a house or flat. In the nature of things, such families had little or no furniture of their own. So the centre advertised for gifts of furniture and had a rota of drivers who could collect second-hand furniture when it was given and then deliver it to the new homes of clients. One day, Prema, one of the Asian women at the centre, announced that she and her two young children had been allocated a council house and were preparing to move. The system swung into action, and within a few days a van was ready to deliver enough basic furniture to enable the family to move in. Tom and Brian were the crew who drove the van on the day of the move. They enjoyed this bit of voluntary work, joked with each other as they drove, and always bought a couple of Yorkie Bars to boost an imagined picture of themselves as international truck drivers. When they arrived at the house Prema and her children were already there, and anxiously on the lookout for the furniture. The van was quickly unloaded, and Tom and Brian helped Prema to arrange it and to make the house habitable. One of the things that struck both young men was that pictures had already been put up on the walls. Some were photographs, some pictures of country scenes, and others were garish portraits of Hindu gods. There on one wall were pictures of Rama, Krishna and Sita. Why was it, Brian wondered, that this made him feel distinctly uneasy? His unease was heightened, not removed, when in another room he saw an equally garish picture of Jesus, sacred heart and all. He asked Prema about the pictures, and why it was that she had gathered together this particular collection. This led to a lengthy conversation which was continued on a subsequent day back at the centre. Prema began by saying how important her religious faith was to her. She prayed regularly, visited the Hindu mandir, or temple, on special festival days, and had the pictures on the walls as a reminder of the significance she attached to sacred things in the daily life of the home as well as on special occasions. Brian (a keenly evangelical Christian) thought this commendable in its way, but found it hard to understand why she should include Jesus along with Rama, Krishna and Sita. With a disarming smile, Prema replied that Krishna. Rama, Sita, the Buddha and Jesus are all the same. All convey something of the wonder of God; all are vehicles of revelation. Brian was shocked. 'Jesus is not like Rama and Krishna,' he said. 'Jesus really is God, the one true revelation through whom people can come to God.' Prema, an intelligent young woman, was a little confused by that last sentence. How could Jesus be at the same time God and the way to God? But she didn't want to engage in arguments of that sort. There was too much discord between people of different religious faiths. That was one reason why she was glad to be able to say that she accepted Jesus, which is what Brian appeared to want her to do. At the same time, of course, she also accepted the Buddha, and Rama and Krishna and Sita. All were paths to God.

Much discussion followed. Brian gradually came to see that what Prema was saying was not 'they are all the same', but 'they are all of value'. And behind that there appeared to be a Hindu view that one incarnation cannot be adequate for all times and all places. In response to Brian's protestations that Jesus is precisely that – the one incarnation for all time and in all places – Prema calmly maintained that an incarnation of God appearing in one particular place and at one stage of human history was limited both culturally and historically. The God who is revealed is not limited; but the vehicle of revelation

28

is. Brian found two things difficult in that. One was her notion that the revelation of God in Jesus Christ could have been limited in its historical and cultural impact by the fact that Jesus of Nazareth lived in first-century Palestine; the other was the distinction being drawn between God, and the person (in his case, Jesus) in whom God is revealed. After several conversations Brian felt, with some frustration, that he had not succeeded in convincing Prema of the truth of his argument. But he understood that what she was saying was that most Hindus believe in one God, although in a rather different way from most Christians. The ultimate expression of God, they believe, cannot be comprehended in a world of space and time, of change and causation. Precisely because of that, there must be intermediaries who appear in particular places at particular times – among them Rama, Krishna and Sita – and Jesus.

In spite of the difficulties he felt with some of the things Prema said, Brian came to appreciate that she was a woman of high moral values and of genuine spirituality. Indeed, her practice of prayer and devotion in the midst of a busy family life and her apparently instinctive sense of dependence upon God appeared to be at least equal and possibly superior to that of most Christians he knew. How was it that her Hindu faith led her to such an impressive standard of religious understanding and practice?

Conversations about whether different religions should be regarded as exclusive, or whether they should be thought of as different paths to the same goal, continued over several weeks. In the course of one of the discussions, somebody suggested that the primary Christian virtue is love, not right opinion. That, too, made Brian think furiously. And when Prema was told of that idea she laughed and said, 'In that case, I must be a good Christian,' and then explained that her name – Prema – means love. None of the others had realized the significance of the name, but when they did they began to reflect in their different ways that linguistic and cultural differences need to be surmounted if true understanding is to be found between religions.

Questions for discussion

1. How would you have answered Prema's assertion that *one* revelation is unlikely to be adequate for all times and all places?

2. Prema's Hindu faith led to an impressive standard of religious understanding and practice. How do you react to this?

See questions 1, 2 on p. 63.

6

An Inter-Faith Marriage

Keith and Mary Bagnell both came from loyal Church of England families, and were proud of it. Their families included a flock of lay readers, several men and women who had been church wardens, two or three priests, and even a bishop. The tradition went back several generations, and almost all their friends and a large number of their relatives were Anglicans. At family gatherings there was always talk about church matters, and people would know the personalities referred to and the distinctive terms used within the community. What happened in the church, who was who and what was what, were of great significance. To some degree their own family reputations rested upon their standing within the church community.

The Bagnells had two children, the eldest of them a delightful and lively daughter, Elizabeth, who was now studying history at a university some two hundred miles away. Keith and Mary were extremely proud of Elizabeth, and since neither had themselves been to university they were appreciative of the opportunities that had come her way. Their picture of university life, Elizabeth suspected, was rather too strongly influenced by television series which featured ancient colleges with green lawns in cloistered courts, gowned dons exuding an air of effortless superiority, and students who appeared little troubled by the need to study. What would they think, Elizabeth wondered in a seminar one day, if they could see this crowded little room with its peeling paint, and the tutor in scruffy jeans and pullover, indistinguishable from many of the students until he intervened in the discussion with his sardonic comments.

Keith and Mary did worry a little about social life at university. Elizabeth, blonde and blue-eyed with a clear fair skin and a lovely figure, was a girl who attracted attention. That had been obvious in the church youth club, but there they knew the boys who clustered around her. Now they had to trust her to her own judgment of the men who undoubtedly would be attracted to her. How would she handle the undoubted blessings and obvious perils of her own good looks? Scarcely veiled questions about boy friends were skilfully deflected in telephone conversations. The parents could only wait patiently to see if and when she would bring someone home to meet them.

It was not until the end of her final year, just before Keith and Mary were due to go to the graduation ceremony, that Elizabeth brought him home. They had probably expected a pleasant young man from the University Anglican Society. They were introduced to Ananda, and it took them a few attempts to get the name right. Ananda (the name, it was explained, is the Sanskrit word for 'bliss') was in his mid-twenties, slim, with large dark eyes, a shaven head and a small pony tail. When they got over their initial shock, they discovered Ananda to be an engaging young man with a great sense of humour and the ability to talk easily about all sorts of things. Their second surprise was still to come. Elizabeth announced that she and Ananda planned to marry within a few months. Keith and Mary had mixed reactions. Ananda seemed pleasant enough; there was nothing about him to which they could reasonably object. But they had only just been introduced, and knew very little about his background. What had most surprised them during the course of the first meal they had shared together (after a brief hiatus when Elizabeth had rushed into the kitchen to explain to her mother that she, like Ananda, had become a vegetarian) was the news that Ananda was a practising Buddhist. That was going to take longer to digest. How would they be able to explain this to their friends and relatives?

The Bagnells were not narrow-minded people, but here was a shock to their cultural and religious assumptions that would take time to assimilate. Their unthinking assumptions that Elizabeth would live the kind of life they had lived, mix with the kind of people they mixed with, and bring her children up in the kind of environment they had known, all seemed to be challenged. Ananda as a friend was one thing. But they were to be married. They could not imagine what adjustments that might require on Elizabeth's part, and they were fearful of how it might affect their relationship with their daughter.

That evening they were able to begin a series of conversations with Elizabeth and Ananda that helped set their minds at rest. It began with Ananda responding to their questions about what it means to be a Buddhist in Britain, and what it is that Buddhists do in the practice of their religion. Since Keith and Mary naturally thought in terms of church-going, and all the other activities associated with that, they at first assumed that being a Buddhist must be a matter of joining an organization and attending something (would it be a temple?) week by week. Ananda explained, with patience and a certain quiet humour, that it was not like that. There was no direct equivalent of the regular church attendance expected of committed Christians. Most British Buddhist groups, he said, focussed chiefly on meditation. He attended a weekly meditation group at his own Buddhist centre on a fairly regular basis, but people came and went, stuck with it if they found meditation helpful, but were not expected to spend time keeping the organization running. There were classes in meditation, open to Buddhists and non-Buddhists alike, and he himself had learned how to meditate at such a class. And for most Buddhists in Britain the local Buddhist centre was a rented hall or set of rooms, not the expensive plant maintained by other faith groups.

To the Bagnells that sounded at once reassuring and surprising. It was very different from the church life they had known. They delicately enquired about belief. Presumably, they asked, Buddhists do believe in God? No, replied Ananda. Few British Buddhists would say that they believed in a personal God, and many would regard that as a positive feature

33

of Buddhism. Buddhists do speak of a transcendental reality, beyond the reach of the world of the senses (sometimes referred to as *nirvana*), and maybe that is what it is that makes Buddhism a religion rather than simply a particular kind of humanism. But they do not believe that a supernatural and all-powerful deity will help them to achieve spiritual progress; that they must do for themselves.

Mary and Keith found that a little difficult. Most of the preaching they had listened to over the years had emphasized the notion that what most needs to be done (the salvation of individuals or societies) could in the end only be done by God. This seemed very different. And the idea of people sitting in silent meditation for an hour or more at a time was also difficult to relate to their own experience of a church-going religion, in which texts were constantly being expounded and people in effect were being told what to believe. If belief, as it seemed to them, was less clear and less important than among Christians, were there other things that were important?

Ananda tried to explain some of the common Buddhist values, expressed in ethical precepts, which included truthfulness, not stealing, and right sexual conduct, but also placed considerable emphasis upon non-violence. The last of these explained not only why many Buddhists are concerned about disarmament and getting rid of nuclear weapons, but also why there seemed to him to be a natural association between Buddhist belief and practice and concern for the environment. In personal terms, non-violence also encouraged most Buddhists to be vegetarians. Essential to it all, he said, was teaching about not clinging to things; realizing that everything around us is impermanent and changing, and therefore trying not to be attached to possessions.

There seemed to be an attractive simplicity about Buddhism, although it did not appear to be easy to accommodate to an acquisitive and violent world, and it clearly made considerable demands upon its adherents. They were not sure how Elizabeth would cope with being married to a Buddhist; would conflicts arise over questions of religious belief and practice? Elizabeth and Ananda had already talked at length about this. The probability was that Elizabeth would retain her Church of England connections. Ananda might go to church with her sometimes. And Elizabeth was interested in attending meditation classes, although she had no intention of becoming a Buddhist. They had some friends who had learned their meditation at a Buddhist centre, but who now regularly attended their local Quaker Meeting. That suggested a compromise that might also be attractive to Elizabeth and Ananda. What especially struck Mary and Keith was how much, and how freely, they had spoken in a positive but non-dogmatic way about religion with their prospective son-in-law. And what a nice chap he was! Elizabeth was doing the right thing.

Questions for discussion

1. How difficult is it to handle the situations that arise when our children marry people whose background is very different from our own?

2. What do you make of the Buddhist values which Ananda explained? Do they seem to you to be complementary, or opposed, to Christian values?

See questions 1, 2 on p. 75, and the comment on p. 45, paragraph 2.

Part 2

Thinking Through the Issues

7

Worship and Prayer

The subject of multi-faith worship has aroused strong feelings among Christians. Some feel that to worship with people who do not make a confession of faith in Jesus Christ is to engage in an act of dangerously misleading syncretism or even of idolatry. Stories of early Christian martyrs whose death resulted from their refusal to make an offering to the emperor has encouraged the view that engaging in worship with people of other faiths is a betrayal of Christian faith. It should be recognized that today's multi-faith worship is rather different, and is likely to be regarded by minority faith groups as an expression of neighbourliness.[4] In our time, temptations to worship the powers that be are presented in subtler forms than that of an invitation to light a candle to the sovereign. What then are the issues for us?

Occasions when people of different faiths worship together (or appear to do so) may be divided into four main categories. One is the inter-faith celebration of the kind Robert found himself explaining to Rebecca (chapter 1, p. 5). A second (perhaps the most common occurrence) is when people visit the worship centre of another faith group, chiefly for observation. A third category, which presents the most difficult issues, is when a service is planned and conducted on an explicitly multi-faith basis; often this will be in connection with a particular civic or national occasion. And fourthly, there is the increasing number of weddings and funerals which gather together congregations made up of people of different faiths sprinkled with a fair representation of atheists and agnostics.

The first category, the inter-faith celebration, is the subject of the first case study, and does not I think present any serious problems. When an inter-faith group or a civic leader decides to stage such a celebration it is often because they wish to demonstrate publicly the work of inter-faith co-operation being undertaken in a particular area or, in the case of the civic leader, to show that members of different ethnic and religious groups can co-operate harmoniously with one another. At such celebrations members of various faith groups will present readings, songs, music and poetry from their traditions. Often there will be a particular theme – the Week of Prayer for World Peace; care of the environment; race relations. Although events of this kind can be very moving, and can help those present to appreciate the wealth of spirituality present in all the major religious traditions, they are not necessarily occasions for people to worship together. Prayers may be included (and if so they should be as simple and non-confessional as possible), but an inter-faith celebration is not the place for corporate prayer or affirmation.

The second kind of inter-faith encounter, in the context of a visit to a place of worship, need not be a problem to those who are fearful of compromising their faith, although the culture shock may be considerable. Most faith groups will welcome the presence at their worship of members of other faiths, and some inter-faith groups will organize such visits as part of their regular programme. Educational visits are increasingly common for students and schoolchildren, and on these occasions members of the host community will usually explain something of the significance of the building and of what goes on in worship. It is also possible for local congregations to organize a visit to a nearby synagogue, temple, gurdwara or mosque, and in return invite their hosts back to observe a Christian service. It can be a salutary experience to ask, what will the visitors make of our worship? How impressive will it appear to a member of another faith group? Will they get the impression that they are in a place of deep spirituality and strong moral concern?

In all these cases, observers are seeing what normally happens in a service. They are not expected to join in worship, unless they especially wish to do so, and what is encountered is therefore not something that is being adjusted to conform to some supposed multi-faith norm. Christian visitors to non-Christian places of worship can expect a warm welcome. The hosts will make plain how pleased they are to have visitors, to show them around, and to explain the significance of things that are done in worship. In addition, refreshments may be offered.

It is also possible to visit many gurdwaras, mosques or temples on a private basis, whether or not worship is actually in progress. There is great fascination in sitting quietly at the back of a mosque at the time of prayer, watching Muslims gather in straight lines, starting from the front of the mosque (not filling up from the back, as most churches do!), and noticing the ways in which the form of worship demonstrates so strongly the brotherhood of Islam; or in sitting at one side in a Hindu temple or Sikh gurdwara to see individuals come in to say their prayers and receive a blessing. The sense of peace and tranquillity, of devotion and prayer is almost palpable.

The issues which may trouble Christian visitors are few, but need to be taken seriously. There is a practical need to recognize the basic courtesies of the tradition – removing shoes on entering temple, gurdwara and mosque; covering the head in gurdwara and synagogue, and sometimes in the mosque (although not required, it is appropriate for women to cover their heads in a temple, as Hindu women usually do). And dressing modestly, in clothes that conceal shoulders and legs and are suitable when sitting on the floor. It may then be necessary to take a decision about how to act in relation to practices of worship. It seems a common courtesy, for example, to bow towards the Guru Granth Sahib in the gurdwara (Sikhs bow to the ground), and Christians need not fear that such an act implies a kind of doctrinal assent to the scriptures of another faith. It may also be the case (even on a private visit) that the visitor will be offered *prasad* (a pleasant semolina-based sweet) in the gurdwara, and again this may be taken as a

41

symbolic offering of Sikh hospitality and of the belief that everyone is to be welcomed to the gurdwara. In the Hindu temple it is customary to offer individual worshippers fruit, nuts or sweets, and this may seem a little more delicate for the Christian visitor, since the fruit may have been offered in worship before images of the gods. The visitor will have to make up her own mind about whether this is to be taken simply as a gesture of hospitality and accepted in that way, or whether it might constitute what the New Testament describes as 'food offered to idols', and so politely declined. But the visit to a place of worship of another faith will almost always open the mind and heart to an appreciation of the spirituality, sincerity and warm hospitality of other faith groups.

The issues about multi-faith worship come to a head with the third category, that of actual multi-faith services. When in December 1991 2,000 clergy of the Church of England supported a letter to *The Times* opposing 'inter-faith prayer and worship' it appeared to be this kind of activity they had in mind. Corporate worship, of the kind Christians are familiar with, is usually engaged in by people with a faith in common. Assumptions about belief ('Jesus is Lord'; 'There is no God but Allah, and Muhammad is his messenger'; 'God is One. . . . the True Name . . . revealed by the grace of the Guru') may, therefore, be expressed in the knowledge that worshippers will hear them as appropriate and meaningful statements of the faith held by members of their own religious community. For this reason it is natural that corporate worship should normally be an activity engaged in by people who have a faith in common, or indeed by those people of religious faith who interpret their religion in broadly similar terms (as with the different emphases of denominations among Christians). This is one reason why corporate worship for schools is such a vexed issue. But should exceptions to this normal practice be allowed?

That the answer to that question is 'yes' becomes apparent when one considers the occasions on which multi-faith worship actually occur. The annual celebration of Commonwealth Day at Westminster Abbey is sometimes held to be an example of multi-faith worship, although in practice that has been more an 'Observance' (what I have described as a 'celebration') than an act of worship. Yet the multi-cultural and multi-religious diversity of the Commonwealth is one of its outstanding and most positive features, and it would be odd to celebrate Commonwealth Day without acknowledging that; it should be possible on such an occasion for people to worship together.[5] More locally, if scouts and guides are to attend a place of worship on St George's Day, or a town is to hold a civic service on Remembrance Sunday, or there is to be a memorial service following a disaster, then it is necessary to recognize the variety of beliefs that are likely to be represented. To do otherwise, and to insist on a purely Christian service when members of other faiths are or would like to be present, would be to indulge in an act remarkable for its absence of Christian charity.

Multi-faith services appear to be most appropriate when those present share a common concern beyond that of their own religious confession. The planning of such a service will require tact and diplomacy, choosing hymns, readings and prayers in which references are more to common human concerns than to a particular faith community. Although a concession to the presence of a multi-faith congregation, this is not a rupturing of Christian traditions. It would not be unusual to use, say, a Jewish prayer – or indeed, the prayer of some other faith – in a Christian service. I doubt whether Methodists object to the adaptation of the beautiful prayer from Hindu scriptures that has come via the Church of South India into the Methodist service for the baptism of infants.[6] And some hymns, including popular hymns for young people such as Sydney Carter's 'One more step along the road I go', are completely neutral in terms of faith claims. This helps what is in any case inevitable in any multi-faith service, that is that worshippers will attribute their own meanings, in the light of their own faith traditions, to material that is used. It could reasonably be argued, of course, in support of the acceptability of this kind of adjustment to a service, that Christian worshippers in any case make their own personal faith assumptions about how to interpret what is said and sung in a regular service. Provided that there is nothing explicitly anti-Christian in a prayer, or song, or reading it is difficult to see why it could not be included.

The problem many Christians have with multi-faith worship is usually to do with services held in a church. In that context, they expect worship to be distinctively Christian, and indeed members of some other faiths may be uneasy if invited to worship in sight of a cross, statues, or pictures. It is perfectly possible, of course, for such services to be held in a community hall or school, or on the premises of another faith community where the choice of material will lie with some other group. In proposing or supporting multi-faith worship on somebody else's premises, Christians need to be aware that the concept of a 'service', consisting of hymns, prayers, scripture readings and a sermon, is peculiarly Christian. A Sikh act of worship in the gurdwara may come closest, with readings from the Guru Granth Sahib, prayers and an address. Normal Muslim worship is quite different, in that the prayers are set prayers in Arabic said to the accompaniment of rhythmic movements, including prostration. Buddhists emphasize meditation, and many Buddhist groups also practise chanting. Hindu worship traditionally has been worship in the home, with visits to temples to make offerings and say prayers as an additional possibility, although some modern Hindu movements and Hindus outside India have adopted forms of congregational worship. Jewish and Christian forms of worship are not so far apart, since Christian worship not surprisingly bears a resemblance to aspects of worship used in the synagogue. But the many differences should encourage Christians planning multi-faith worship to avoid the readily-made assumption that members of all faiths will share broadly the same ideas about what might constitute 'worship'. If multi-faith worship is to be used on occasions of broad national concern, then great sensitivity and restraint will have to be exercised by all those involved.

The fourth category is likely to become increasingly common. In our multi-faith society weddings and funerals may be expected more and more to include people from different faith communities, as well as those who have no religious faith. It is already possible to adapt a marriage service so that, for example, it can accommodate the needs of a church member who is marrying an atheist or an agnostic. The church member can make explicitly Christian vows: the non-believing partner can make vows which are adapted to avoid hypocrisy on his or her part. In a similar way it is possible to adapt a marriage service for a church member and a person of another faith. If a reciprocal service were to be held, similar concessions would need to be made to the Christian participant. So far as funerals are concerned, sensitivity to non-Christian worshippers might be regarded as an essential courtesy. But since so many funerals now take place in a crematorium or cemetery chapel, and since anyone may conduct such a service in any way they wish, the possibilities for multi-faith worship at funerals are likely to become increasingly common and in all probability will become more and more fascinating in their variety.

Questions for discussion

1. If asked to make a brief Christian contribution to an inter-faith celebration, could you suggest something that would encapsulate what Christian faith is about?

2. What experiences have people had of visits to other faith places of worship? If there is little experience in the group, should some visits be planned?

3. If your church were asked to host a multi-faith service for a celebration of Commonwealth Day, or to mark the millennium, would you be able to suggest songs, hymns and readings which would not give offence to other faith communities?

8

Silence in Worship

The issue about a yoga class (chapter 2) and a conversation with Ananda, a Buddhist, (chapter 6) raised questions about the place of meditation and silence in worship. Discussions in the property committee about whether or not to have a yoga class on church premises led to positive conclusions: it was hoped that members of such a class might find their way into the church's worship, especially if silence were made a more significant feature of that; and the thought was expressed that talk about a yoga class on the premises might encourage church members to start a meditation group which itself could then influence what happened in worship. Elizabeth Bagnell had already expressed her interest in attending a meditation class at a Buddhist centre, and both she and Ananda had thought how good it would be if they could find ways of combining their different religious practices.

It might seem curious that in those contexts it was discussion about yoga, originally a practice of Indian religions, that led to a desire to revive practices that are also an important part of Christian spirituality. Whether in private prayer or public worship, silence and meditation can provide effective ways of deepening and enriching Christian worship. Perhaps the techniques of modern communications have influenced our church worship too much in the direction of entertainment, with the idea that people's attention must be diverted and held all the time. That leads too readily to the assumption that the one thing to be avoided at all costs is silence. Yet silent reflection and meditation have played a large part in spirituality within many religious traditions, including those of Christianity. Could it be that Christians might regain an interest in silent worship and prayer through an acquaintance with the practices of other religions?

Before meditation can become a useful part of either corporate worship or private prayer and reflection, practice and guidance will be required. Being still and focussing the mind is not something that comes naturally to most of us in a world of rush and constantly changing images. One of the benefits sought by people who attend yoga classes is the ability to be still and to relax, with body and mind in control. It is this that has been taught in systems of yoga for centuries, and there is no reason why Christians should not benefit from that teaching, adapting it to the uses of Christian prayer and worship,

The teaching of meditation is likely to begin with advice and encouragement about how to be quiet and relaxed. It is helpful to sit with a straight back in a posture that can be held comfortably for a considerable time – with practice it is not difficult to sit completely still for half-an-hour, and even a whole hour can be managed quite easily after a while, daunting as that may seem at the outset. Control of body and mind, as well as relaxation, can then be encouraged by slow, steady breathing. Few of us would ever pause to think about breathing. It seems far too natural for that. But try to notice your breathing. Breathe in and out, slowly and deliberately. Count, or look at the second hand of a clock, while you do it: breathe in for, say six or eight seconds; hold your breath for ten or twelve seconds; breathe out for a further eight seconds. And then pause for a moment before starting the process again! Then in your mind run through some short prayers or verses as you do so. You will think of appropriate prayers, but the following may get you started:

O God, of your goodness give me yourself, for only in you have I all.

Holy Spirit, fill me with inspiration and creativity.

God of love, empower us to love other people.

It is also possible, and initially may be easier, to use single words or very short phrases to accompany the rhythm of breathing, and for the Christian, words and phrases with a

Christian resonance may be the most helpful: 'Jesus, Lord'; 'grace and peace' (I Corinthians 1.3); 'do not be anxious' (Matthew 6.25), are examples. The reader will be able to think of many more.

Alternatively, slow down the mental recitation of a longer prayer (perhaps the Lord's Prayer) by fitting the phrases of the prayer into a pattern of slowly breathing in, holding the breath, and breathing out again. Breathe in to 'Our Father, who art in heaven'; hold the breath to 'Hallowed be thy Name, thy kingdom come, thy will be done, on earth as it is in heaven'; breathe out to 'Give us this day our daily bread. And forgive us our trespasses, as we forgive those who trespass against us.' Then pause for a moment! Breathe in to 'And lead us not into temptation', hold the breath to 'But deliver us from evil. For thine is the kingdom, the power and the glory', and finally breathe out to, 'For ever and ever. Amen.' Some may prefer to use a favourite verse from scripture as the basis for meditation, or some other writing that you find inspiring. An obvious Christian mantra on which to reflect is Paul's description of the 'harvest of the Spirit' as:

love, joy, peace,

patience, kindness, goodness,

faithfulness, gentleness and self-control' (Galatians 5.22–23).

A significant part of meditation may be a reflection upon some urgent social or political issue, or a local problem, and the consideration of whether and in what ways we can do anything to help.

Suitably adapted for corporate use, guidance of this kind might also encourage a congregation to spend part of an act of worship in silence, and so to enter into a fresh experience of worship. Meditation is likely to be much shorter when it is initially used within acts of public worship, and few congregations are likely to emulate the inspired insight of the Book of Revelation when it declared that 'there was silence in heaven for about half an hour' (Revelation 8.1). But silence for several minutes within an act of worship can be a wonderful opportunity to enrich worship by encouraging people to pray and think for themselves for a sustained period while the barrage of words is silenced.

Questions for discussion

1. What part does silence play in your church's worship?

2. Christian meditation, like yoga, is not concerned with asking for blessings. Is this a positive or negative aspect of meditation?

3. Practise the relaxation, breathing and silent prayer described on pp. 48–49.

9

Scripture

The great religious traditions cherish and honour their scriptures. Not all religions place quite the same degree of importance upon the collection of writings which for them constitutes scripture; but in almost all cases the writings are revered, frequently referred to in discussion and debate, and used to define the tradition of which they are part. In many cases what is found in the holy book or books of a religion is believed to be revelation, and therefore in some sense a major authority for what is to be believed and practised. So it is with the Bible among Christians. Sunday by Sunday public readings from Old and New Testaments form part of the worship attended by millions of people. No doubt what they make of them varies greatly, but the influence of biblical readings among churchgoers is likely to be considerable. Sometimes what is read is expounded with sensitivity and skill. If that is not done, the readings may create, consciously or unconsciously, a strange combination of ideas and images. For the Bible, in common with the scriptures of some other traditions, poses many problems. The first book in this series discussed many of the issues that arise in reading and studying the Bible,[7] and they will not be rehearsed here. But questions about the authority and interpretation of scriptures become even more complex in inter-faith discussions.

The issues become particularly difficult when scriptures of different religions have material in common. What for the Christian is the Old Testament is for the Jew the Hebrew Bible, although the interpretation of the common scriptures varies considerably. The Muslim's *Qur'an* has some material which is also found in the Hebrew Bible and the New Testament. What are we to make of that? If we were to claim that the New Testament has a priority over the Old Testament because it comes later in time, then should we not also have to acknowledge that the *Qur'an*, which emerged some five hundred years later than the New Testament, has priority over both its predecessors? Christians have often claimed that Christian faith supersedes Judaism as the later revelation. Readings of the New Testament, in which Old Testament texts are interpreted as pointing towards the Christian revelation, are frequently employed as 'proof' texts for this position. But Christians who wish to take that position with regard to Judaism must beware. For a very similar view is taken by Muslims of both Christian and Jewish scriptures when they claim that Islam fulfils and supersedes both Judaism and Christianity. Christians cannot have it both ways. If Christianity supersedes Judaism, then by the same argument Islam supersedes Christianity as the third of the three great revelations.

If this all seems a little too complex, let me say that the questions are raised because of the way in which they bring into focus inter-faith discussions about scripture. On what grounds are we to choose between what may appear to be competing truth-claims in different scriptures? The religious believer who produces proof texts in order to assert the superiority of his or her faith may then be outbid by a proof text from another faith. And the process is likely to become very negative. To say in effect, 'my religion is true because it says that it is true,' is not helpful. All religions claim to be the vehicles of truth. Christians claim that their faith is a response to the final revelation. But Muslims make a similar claim for their faith. And even followers of a religion which appears to place much less emphasis upon scripture, such as Buddhism, also believe that their scriptures and traditions are the vehicles of the truth about the human condition and the appropriate religious response to it.

Of course, scriptures do have different force in different religious traditions (even between Protestants and Catholics). As Simon and Penelope discovered (chapter 4, p. 22), Muslims believe the *Qur'an* to be the unmediated word of God when it is read in Arabic. That is a logical position. If you believe your scriptures are God's direct word, then you cannot translate them and still retain that immediate sense of 'the word of God'. Muslim children are often expected to learn Arabic, even when it is not the language spoken by their families or in the country in which they live, because only by doing so can they hear the *Qur'an* in its original voice and join fully in Muslim worship. Christians have never taken that view. Indeed, given the complexity of Christian scriptures, it would be virtually impossible to hold to such a view. So far as we know, Jesus spoke in Aramaic; he may have known some Hebrew (when he read the scriptures in the synagogue, was that the Hebrew text or a translation?); but our records of his words are in Greek. They have since been translated into a vast number of languages, and even if we confine ourselves to English translations we have to admit that there are considerable variations between them. We know that to translate from one language to another is to change what is said, even if only in subtle ways. Which of the English translations, then, could be regarded as 'the word of God'? Or should we encourage Christians to read the Greek text of the New Testament and the Hebrew text of the Old Testament? For those who are the most serious exponents of the texts and the tradition, that remains a reasonable expectation. But we can hardly expect it of congregations as a whole.

If we take an open view of the matter, we have to accept that scriptures live in communities, that they are the products of the lives of religious communities, and that therefore the scriptures of one faith community cannot be the only or even the most appropriate yardstick by which to judge another. In interpreting Christian scriptures in matters that have to do with the faith of other people, we have to exercise great sensitivity. We know how important scripture, and especially the New Testament, is for Christian life. We would not wish to play that down in conversations with members of other faith communities, but we do need to remember that scriptures arise in particular social and historical contexts. The interpretation of biblical texts is a difficult and complex business, and the mere quoting of a text in isolation is never likely to be the most appropriate way of responding to the treasures of other faiths.

In the light of that, and conscious of the fact that there is not space here for a thorough discussion of texts, let us turn by way of illustration to some biblical passages. John 14.6 is often quoted as a key text, with Jesus saying to his closest disciples: 'I am the way, the truth and the life; no one comes to the Father except by me.' For many Christians that has seemed to support the belief that the only way to God is through Jesus; he is the only way to salvation for all people in all places and at all times. What the text also suggests is that, as we know on other grounds, Christian faith was widely regarded as 'the way' – that is, as a commitment to follow a particular way of life in response to the call of Christ. In context, the words are addressed to Thomas, who has asked, 'Lord, we do not know where you are going, so how can we know the way?' In that sense, the words of Jesus are explicitly addressed to followers who in response to a question about what they are to do are told that the disciple is to follow the way of the teaching and example of Jesus.

There is also a hint here of the concealment of the nature of God, and the belief that it is through the *logos* (the self-disclosure of God) that he is made known. In John's Gospel, the *logos* (translated as 'word') is applied to Jesus. But it has wider implications, for the *logos*, the word of God, is in biblical terms what is spoken at creation, through the prophets, and, indeed, at other times and places. None of this is to deny the force of the words, 'I am the way, the truth and the life' when addressed to Christians; but it does suggest that to take them from their original context and apply them to people of many other religious faiths in other cultures and contexts may not be the most obvious interpretation of the verse.

A second common 'proof text' is found in Acts 4.12: 'There is no salvation through anyone else; in all the world no other name has been granted to mankind by which we can be saved.' That seems clear enough. Or is it? The words are those of Peter, who is responding to the 'rulers of the people and elders' in Jerusalem who have asked by what authority Peter and John healed a sick man. It should be recognized that the word 'salvation' in the gospels – as in the Old Testament – refers most often to deliverance from some practical calamity, which may include sickness. Peter is defending the act of healing a sick person 'in the name of Jesus'. Is it not then at least a little curious to take the words out of their context and use them to assert or imply that non-Christian religious faith is without value?

The answer to that last question may depend upon the degree to which a person uses the words of the Bible as though they were spoken directly by God and are applicable to any situation and any time or place. At the very least, that seems a strange way of using biblical texts in relation to complex modern issues. It is possible to oppose the texts cited above with examples of Jesus commending the faith of people who were not his followers and not Jews – the Syro-Phoenician woman (Mark 7.24–30) and the centurion (Luke 7.1–10). Even so, it is unlikely that a direct application of biblical texts to inter-faith issues that did not exist in the world of Jesus of Nazareth will provide any lasting solutions to today's questions.

The need for sensitivity to people of other faiths when reading the New Testament is nowhere more acute than with regard to Jews and Judaism. In recent years, and in light of the *sho'ah* (or holocaust), both Christian and Jewish scholars have paid increasing attention to the roots of anti-Jewish sentiment in Christian societies. It is clear that some major figures in the early church (Chrysostom, Hippolytus) were virulently anti-Jewish, accusing Jews of their own times of murdering God's son.[8] Sadly, such attitudes have persisted right up to the present time. And there is a connection with scripture which is all the more insidious because it is rarely noticed. There is a popular, but of course mistaken, impression that Christianity and the Christian church were somehow already in existence during the lifetime of Jesus of Nazareth. That has been encouraged by the way in which in the writing of the Gospels, between thirty-five and perhaps ninety years after the death of Jesus, the early church put together accounts of his life and ministry and their own later concerns. The unsuspecting reader therefore may be led to believe that 'the Jews' were indeed a separate group of people. John's Gospel, generally assumed to have been the last to be written, refers sixty-seven times to 'the Jews' by way of contrast to Jesus and his followers. Yet a moment's thought reminds us that Jesus and his disciples were also Jews. Arguments between Jesus and the scribes and Pharisees were arguments *within* a single religious community, in much the same way as churches today have their internal debates. In their historical context they do not reflect a Christian criticism of Judaism.

That historical shift in common readings of the New Testament has particularly serious consequences in the accounts of the trial and execution of Jesus. It is clear that the Roman authorities were responsible for the death of Jesus, and there are a number of theories about why they took the decision they did. But the recording of the events of trial and crucifixion have been written up in such a way as to give the impression that 'the Jews' were responsible. The supposed cry of the crowd to Pilate, 'His blood be on us and on our children' (Matthew 27.25) has rung out down the centuries as Christians have applied the words literally, and far too often have held all Jews of all time responsible for the death of Jesus. Careful and accurate exposition of scriptures, aided by all the scholarship that is available, is required if readings from scriptures are to help rather than hinder inter-faith understanding.

Questions for discussion

1. How important is it for the Christian reader of the Gospels to be aware of differences between material which reflects the life and teaching of the early church and words which may reasonably be attributed to Jesus?

2. What do you understand by the phrase 'the word of God'? Discuss the different way it is used, and consider whether it is misleading to call the Bible 'the word of God'.

3. Why does the New Testament sometimes give the impression that 'the Jews' were a people separate from Jesus and his disciples?

10

Similarities and Differences

The difficulties we encounter in trying to establish clear scriptural views about other faiths lead on to the question of whether there is any way of assessing the competing truth claims of different faiths. At the outset it is important to recognize that all the major faiths encompass great varieties of practice and belief. One of the reasons why the phrase 'comparative religions' has fallen out of use is that scholars have recognized the impossibility of comparing one major religion with another. It is possible to compare, say, ecstatic dance and worship as found in some specific Christian and Hindu communities, or to compare attitudes to divorce among Baptists in the southern states of the USA with those of Sunni Muslims in Pakistan. It is a different matter altogether to make grand comparisons about what all Muslims, all Christians, or all Hindus do, or think, or believe. Within each of the major faiths there will be vast differences between what members of the same religious faith practise and believe, just as there will be significant differences historically between what people of faith believe today compared with what their forebears believed at different stages of the past. We know, for example, that when we make statements about what are the most important elements in Christian faith and life, there will always be other Christians who will disagree with us. So also generalizations about people of other faiths will be equally misleading. There are varieties of belief and practice among Muslims, as there are among Hindus and Buddhists and Jews.

One consequence of such variety is the difficulty of knowing what, if anything, constitutes the essential elements of a religious tradition. What is it that constitutes the essence of Christianity? In answer to that question, many Christians would say something about belief in Jesus Christ as the Son of God, as the one who is believed to be the unique revelation of God.

58

Some may wish to extend a belief-based answer by claiming that acceptance of the historic creeds is an essential badge of a Christian – although that begs the question of how one is to interpret the creeds. Other Christians will say that the essence of Christianity has to be more than a credal formula, a *statement* about belief that anyone could make. They will argue that at its heart Christianity has to do with following a 'way', by translating into contemporary life the example and teaching of Jesus of Nazareth. Others again would claim that the essence of Christianity is bound up with acceptance of the authority and teaching of the church. To think about what might constitute the essence of Christianity is to recognize the various possible alternative answers that in all sincerity could be given to a simple question.

A question that arises again and again has to do with revelation. Most of the great religions agree that God, or ultimate reality, is wrapped in mystery. The idea of a *transcendent* God is of a God who is beyond and greater than the world we apprehend through our senses. Yet it is claimed that God is known in mystical experience, or through the events of history. God is mysteriously distant and yet also somehow present in the life of the world. Each of the great religions has its own way of explaining how a transcendent God could be revealed, and known, in a changing and transitory world. For example, Islam teaches that God [*Allah*] spoke through an intermediary to the prophet Muhammad, who dictated the words he heard. Those words, spoken and heard in Arabic, became the *Qur'an.* So for the Muslim, the transcendent God who is otherwise unknowable makes his will known through the written word of the *Qur'an.* Christianity, for all its variety, has a common view that what most needs to be known about God has been revealed in the person of Jesus Christ. Clearly, there are considerable differences between a revelation contained in a scripture (the *Qur'an*) and a revelation contained in the life and teaching of a person (Jesus Christ). Christians

59

are not always sufficiently clear about such a distinction. Many Christians seem to think that their revelation is the Bible. It is not so. The Christian revelation is the word of God, spoken in creation, spoken through the great prophets, but supremely contained in the life and teaching of Jesus. The Bible is the vehicle of and witness to revelation, much as Muhammad is the vehicle of and witness to the revelation of the *Qur'an*. For the Christian, the revelation itself is Jesus Christ.

In Hindu traditions there is teaching about a series of incarnations of the great God, Vishnu. The God who is the creator and sustainer of life, it is said, reveals himself at critical times in a series of *avataras* (*avatara* means 'one who comes down'). The best known of the *avataras* are Rama and Krishna, who play a very important part in Hindu devotional religion. But for Hindus, as Prema explained (chapter 5, pp. 25–29), it makes sense to think of a series of *avataras*, because then the incarnation is acknowledged to be related to a particular time and place. The world changes through time and in different places. If God reveals himself directly in personal form, then that revelation, the Hindu will argue, must be conditioned by the culture, society and historical period in which it appears. So there are many revelations, and Hindus are usually happy to acknowledge that Jesus and Buddha may be counted among them.

In this brief discussion of revelation we have come across one of the most contentious issues in inter-faith debate. Religions agree about the existence of a transcendent reality, or God. But they have their different ways of understanding how a mysterious and transcendent God is to be known; how an eternal reality can be encountered in a transient world. Beliefs about revelation through scriptures, prophets, incarnation, or *avataras* are necessarily different, and by many believers are thought therefore to be exclusive. Most traditions will have texts or teaching asserting the truth of their own particular revelation, and sometimes such texts (as in chapter 9 above) are regarded as evidence for the unique value of one religion over against others (chapter 1, p. 7).

In Christian writing about relationships with people of other faiths much has been made of a distinction between three different approaches: the exclusive; the inclusive; and the pluralist. The exclusive approach is the one which says in effect, Christian faith is the absolute or final truth; other religious faiths can at best be inferior; at the worst, they may be positively misleading (a view taken by Hendrik Kraemer and Karl Barth). The inclusive approach allows for the truth found in other religious traditions, but maintains that the final truth is to be found in Christ. This view has been propounded in one way or another by many distinguished Catholic writers, such as Raymond Panikkar, who illustrated the approach by the title of a book, *The Unknown Christ of Hinduism*, in which it was claimed that the best of Hinduism may be regarded as a veiled, or preparatory, form of Christian teaching. The pluralist approach, exemplified by John Hick in *God and the Universe of Faiths* and many other writings, takes the view that the great religions of the world are all possible channels of true revelation.[9]

All three of these are Christian approaches to other religions. They have been much debated, but it can reasonably be claimed that they illustrate the range of possible Christian responses to other faiths. More recently, however, it has been suggested that there is a problem common to all three. They are all concerned, in one way or another, with the question of whether salvation is available and effective in other religions than Christianity. But 'salvation' is a peculiarly Christian concern, and so the question is raised as to whether it is appropriate to judge other religions on what is deemed to be their ability to deliver something in which they may have little interest.[10] A religion such as Buddhism has different concerns (which Buddhists also believe to be universally valid) but the question of whether or not Buddhism is a 'path to salvation' in Christian terms is not one of them (chapter 6, p. 34) That does not mean that Buddhism does not have a significant contribution to make to wider religious understanding. In response to that kind of difficulty, it might be helpful for Christians to think more about the emphasis upon the love of God as a process, rather than upon static views of being, sonship, and salvation. How God's love may be understood and declared would seem to be a more important question than whether one credal formula is superior to another.[11]

These are difficult and extremely important questions. Much has been written about them in the last thirty years or so, and whole libraries could be stocked with the resulting books. There is not space here to do more than mention some of the major issues. Two thoughts might lead to useful further discussion. One is from Wilfred Cantwell Smith, a distinguished American scholar, who drew attention to a possible conflict between the moral and intellectual facets of Christian relationships with people of other faiths. On a moral level, he pointed out, Christians emphasize reconciliation, unity, harmony, and brotherhood, whilst on an intellectual level, if they take the exclusivist view, they deny the value of other people's beliefs. He wrote: 'It is morally not possible actually to go out into the world and say to devout, intelligent, fellow human beings: "We are saved and you are damned", or, "We believe that we know God, and we are right; you believe that you know God, and you are totally wrong." This is intolerable from merely human standards. It is doubly so from Christian ones.'[12]

The second thought is from a British (and Anglican) scholar, Kenneth Cragg, who suggested that the most important thing in Christian mission is not to increase numbers of converts or to increase the geographical spread of Christians, but to encourage, among Christians as well as others, 'the increase of the Christlike person'. As Christians we would do well to keep that in mind if we try to assess the truth claims of different faiths by way of comparison with Christian beliefs.

Questions for discussion

1. What do *you* think is essential to Christian faith?

2. Is personal salvation the main goal of Christian faith? If so, why? If not, why not?

3. Which of the three approaches outlined on p. 61 comes closest to your own view, and why?

11

Race and Community Relations

Questions about inter-faith relations have taken on a new urgency in Britain's modern multi-cultural society. Although it can be argued that in legal terms Britain has been a multi-cultural society since the nineteenth century, it is since the end of the Second World War that substantial communities of people of many faiths – Muslims, Sikhs, Hindus, Jains, as well as Jews and Christians – have come to be established in Britain (Buddhists are an exception, in that most British Buddhists do not come from different ethnic groups). There *are* white Anglo-Saxon Muslims, Sikhs, and Hindus, but the great majority of people practising these religions still have links with immigrant communities which originated in India, Pakistan and Bangladesh. At a time when adherence to Christian churches has declined sharply, this has dramatically changed the map of British religions. When we speak of religion in present-day Britain, we can no longer only speak of Christianity.

In the teaching of religion in schools we have moved from scripture (or divinity), through religious instruction or religious knowledge, to religious education or religious studies. A lot of people have difficulty keeping up with the changes in terminology, and the pernicious effects of out-of-date attitudes to the teaching and study of religions create obvious problems for schools. Many politicians and parents seem to be unable to escape from a cocoon of ignorance in which they think that religion is taught and studied only for purposes of propaganda. But the different titles reflect changes in content which are the result of the considerable transformation religion has undergone in British society. In teaching religious education schools are now required by law 'to reflect the fact that religious traditions in Great Britain are in the main Christian, whilst taking account of the other principal religions represented in Great Britain'. For the first time, therefore, some

64

of the teaching of religion in schools must by law relate to non-Christian religious traditions. In spite of that, it is regrettable that those who have framed the law appear not to have understood that the modern study of religions is a proper – and rigorous – academic subject, and not simply a vehicle for conveying beliefs of particular communities. It is to be hoped that the sensitive and informed teaching of a range of religious traditions will improve understanding not only of religion, but also of people whose cultural and ethnic backgrounds are different from the majority.

The history of people of other faiths in Britain shows that whilst there has been hospitality and tolerance extended to them, there has also been much prejudice. Jewish refugees entering Britain in fairly small numbers at the end of the nineteenth and beginning of the twentieth century were initially allowed free entry into the country (although the Alien's Act of 1905 was then introduced as the first piece of modern legislation designed to limit the entry of people of a particular background). Those Jewish refugees, fleeing from persecution in eastern Europe, were allowed entry, but also encountered considerable prejudice. Their differences, in clothing, language, culture, religion, were all held to pose problems for the majority community. Yet they were accommodated into British society fairly quickly, and it is touching to hear Jewish people who fled from Nazi-occupied Europe in the late nineteen-thirties testifying to the welcome they received in this country at that time. It is also fascinating to see how closely the criticisms of post-1945 New Commonwealth immigrants mirrored the criticism of Jewish refugees fifty years earlier. They too were different in culture and dress and language and religion, in their food and their family structures. Looking back, we see that the problem in both cases had much to do with stereotyping.

Stereotyping is one of the major problems underlying racial prejudice, and it also contributes to religious prejudice. To see all members of a particular faith as essentially the same is to stereotype them, and so to be unable to recognize the inevitable differences that exist between individuals. In the West today it has become commonplace for people to refer to Islamic fundamentalism as though all Muslims are fundamentalists. In fact, of course, there are wide differences of interpretation among Muslims, as among those who belong to other religions. Some Muslims are much more open and relaxed about religious belief and practice than others. Some take quite liberal views of their traditions. To think of all Muslims as fundamentalists is to stereotype them in an unhelpful and misguided way. Jews have also provided targets for stereotyping. You have only to read Shakespeare's *The Merchant of Venice* (written, incidentally, when Jews were not legally allowed to be in England) to feel the force of European Christian stereotyping of Jews. But it has happened in much more recent times. Indeed, the blanket condemnation of all Jews by the Nazis in the horrors of the *sho'ah* was an extreme but telling example of how terrible the consequences of stereotyping can be. To put ourselves in the place of those who suffer from the gross caricatures which suggest that *all* Jews, *all* Muslims, *all* French people, *all* Germans are necessarily the same is to recognize the iniquity of it. Are all British people like the occasional groups of football hooligans who create mayhem on the continent? Are all Christians like those who have persecuted people of other religious faiths, or burned witches at the stake?

We would not ourselves wish to be stereotyped, but to be judged as the people we are. In our relations with people of other faiths, we should do no less for them. And the most effective way of ridding ourselves of stereotypes is to get to know people of other faiths. Knowing them as friends or acquaintances, appreciating the paradoxes that they and we live with, and learning what we can about their traditions and practices will move us away from caricatures. Penelope and Simon made an effort to know their Muslim neighbours. They bought and read an English translation of the *Qur'an*; they read and observed what they could about Islamic faith and practice; they showed an interest in the family'; and their efforts were rewarded (chapter 4, p. 24).

In her conversation with Robert, Rebecca saw the connection between ways of approaching people of other faiths and good community relations (chapter 1, p. 8). They both recognized how particular theological positions can so easily militate against good relationships with people of other faiths. Those who are dismissive of other people's beliefs on theological grounds are likely to have great difficulty in giving those same people appropriate respect and understanding in day-to-day relationships. An assumption that a neighbour's faith is fundamentally wrong may be taken as an expression of contempt for their culture and their racial and ethnic identity. British Christians have been better at developing, albeit slowly, a respect for differences found among people of Afro-Caribbean background than among those whose background is in South Asia. The likeliest reason for that is that Afro-Caribbeans in Britain are most often Christians, whilst Asians are most often from other religious traditions.

With regard to race and community relations, as with other issues, we come back to the underlying question of what might be an appropriate Christian response to people of other faiths. Many Christians take the view that they have an obligation to try to convert the other person to faith in Jesus Christ. That is ultimately what they need, it is thought, and what will be best for them. As we followed John's experiences in thinking through issues about Jews and Jesus, we noticed how initially he assumed that conversion was the right thing to aim for, but that after discussions with David and Ted he concluded that there might be more to be gained by increasing understanding between the faiths than by encouraging people to move from one faith to another (chapter 3). When a person's faith is bound up with their family relationships and community identity, we should think very hard about the consequences of encouraging people to move out of one world of faith and into another. We have noticed that the Gospels represent Jesus as showing little concern with that kind of movement, and much more concern for what is in people's hearts (chapter 9, p. 55). There will be occasions when we shall need to do the same.

Questions for discussion

1. Should religious education encourage pupils to think analytically about religions? Or should it aim at encouraging belief?

2. How can we avoid stereotyping people whose religion, culture or language is different from ours?

3. Is it possible to affirm a person's racial and ethnic identity if at the same time we maintain that their religious faith is fundamentally mistaken?

12

Moral Issues

Matters of belief will seem to many people (including not a few religious believers) to be remote and esoteric concerns. But everybody is concerned about morality, in one way or another. Why people behave the way they do, and how they should behave, are matters of great media interest and of public concern. There is a widespread view that religions have a special responsibility to instil moral values, and when those who profess a religious faith are deemed to be acting immorally, then the cry of 'hypocrisy' rings through the land.

In the late nineteenth century Rudyard Kipling no doubt was reflecting a common European view when he wrote:

Ship me somewhere east of Suez, where the best is like the worst,
Where there aren't no Ten Commandments and a man can raise a thirst.

The idea that morality ended as one left the Suez Canal and headed east was one of those strange but compelling perceptions which went with the experiences of powerful colonial nations. The feelings of superiority which in part justified the conquest and rule of other countries fed assumptions about moral superiority, and coloured the lenses through which the European perceived the rest of the world. One of the consequences of that way of seeing the world beyond Europe was the widespread view that the peoples of Asia, Africa and the Middle East were deficient spiritually and morally. Like some of the other hidden but significant relics of colonialism, that way of looking at religious faiths and moral systems found beyond Europe continues to simmer in the unconscious minds of Europeans.

It was never true, of course. Just as the great religious systems of Asia have existed longer than the Christianity of Europe, so too there have been ethical systems bound up with the religions and exerting great influence on people and

69

societies. East of Suez the Hindus in India had long known the five precepts that provided a basis for morality: non-violence, celibacy (outside of marriage), not stealing, speaking the truth, and not coveting. Buddhism shared the first four of those; not coveting was so closely bound up with the central Buddhist teaching about not clinging to possessions that it was not made a separate precept (chapter 6, p. 34). There in Asia, for at least six hundred years before Christ, there had existed ethical precepts remarkably similar to the moral rules included in the ten commandments.

The last of the three great Semitic religions, Islam, has clear ethical teaching, set out not only in the *Qur'an* but also in *hadith* (traditions) and *sunnah* (the practices of the prophet). In a passage that bears similarities to the ten commandments, the *Qur'an* says: 'Serve no other gods besides Allah ... Your Lord has enjoined you to worship none but Him, and to show kindness to your parents ... Give to the near of kin their due, and also to the destitute and the wayfarers ... You shall not commit adultery ... You shall not kill any man whom Allah has forbidden you to kill, except for a just cause ... Do not interfere with the property of orphans ... Give full measure when you measure, and weigh with even scales ... Do not walk proudly on the earth. You cannot cleave the earth, nor can you rival the mountains in stature' (*Qur'an* 17.21–37, translated by N. J. Dawood).

It was the Jews, of course, whose 'law' books, or Torah, provided a wealth of rules and commandments; and much more besides. Some very orthodox Jews still take the view that all the commandments should be taken literally and applied to present day situations; many accept that some of the rules which were appropriate to a desert community many centuries ago cannot be applied directly to modern issues. In doing that, they are recognizing, as most Christians do, that there has to be selection and interpretation in applying such commandments to life today. From time to time public figures will call for closer adherence to the ten commandments. Rarely do they pause to explain what they think that will mean. Read them through again (Exodus 20.3–17) and you will see the problems. The first three have to do with religious observance: not making carved images; not worshipping gods other than Yahweh; and not making wrong use of the name of the Lord. Whilst all three can be interpreted, they could not simply be applied directly to modern society. The next two are also primarily religious in intent, although they have social significance: keep the sabbath holy – 'that day you must not do any work'; and 'Honour your father and your mother' – a religious commandment, because that is the way the traditions were preserved and transmitted. So when politicians and archbishops call for a return to the ten commandments, do they mean that we should refuse to open or patronize shops or to drive cars on Sundays?

Probably they have in mind the more directly ethical commandments which follow the first five. The first of these, 'Do not commit murder', seems plain enough. Even so, we have to recognize that most Jews and Christians have taken that to mean 'you shall not kill without the sanction of the State'. Observing the commandment has not inhibited State killing, as in the case of capital punishment or in warfare. The second of the five ethical commandments – 'Do not commit adultery' – is the one people in the media have heard of, and so is probably the one commandment which, whilst widely ignored in society as a whole, can be broken by a public figure only with great risk. Yet underlying the hypocrisy which often accompanies 'disclosures' about people's private lives in the Press, there is an awareness of the importance of right sexual relations and stable families for society as a whole. Then there is 'Do not steal', a rule accepted by most people except burglars and unprincipled financiers, but clearly important wherever people live together in communities. That is followed by 'Do not give false evidence against your neighbour', originally envisaging a hearing of a complaint within a fairly small community.

71

Interpretation of that ninth commandment today might lead to the thought that stereotyping or misrepresenting the religion of our neighbour could be an infringement of what the law intends.

The last of the ten commandments is the one that says, 'Do not covet'. That might be thought especially interesting, since a return to a more serious application of the commandments to public life could herald a widespread public demand to ban the advertising industry and the whole economic system which is built around it. In calling for a return to a closer observance of the ten commandments public figures owe us the courtesy of saying precisely what they mean, and whether they have in mind the direct and thoroughgoing application of all or only some of them. We can recognize the importance of what the commandments are after – a personal constraint in community life which places our own wants within a wider framework, and matches our desires and our duties, our rights and our obligations. If we glance back at the precepts shared by Hindus and Buddhists (non-violence, celibacy outside of marriage, not stealing, telling the truth, and not coveting) we shall see how close they are in intention to the moral commandments of Jews, Christians and Muslims. But we still have to interpret and apply the particular moral rules we have inherited.

One particular illustration of this may be taken from 'You shall not commit murder'. In applying that to warfare a minority of Christians have taken the words literally and refused to participate in warfare or in service in the armed forces. The pacifist tradition is an honourable one among Christians. But the majority have conceded that there is a duty to defend the State, and so have agreed to a set of principles in the 'Just War' theory, many of which are also enshrined in international law. They include such provisions as only going to war to defend the State, not attacking non-combatants, and not using more force than is necessary to bring a war to a conclusion – a series of rules designed to mitigate the worst horrors of war. Muslims have done something similar in regard to their command 'not to kill any man . . . ' They, too, agree that a nation should only go to war for defence or to oppose a tyrant, should use minimal force, and should have respect for non-combatants and prisoners.

Buddhists have often been distinguished by the seriousness with which they have applied the precept of *ahimsa*, or non-violence (chapter 6, p. 34). After the Second World War several Buddhist groups from south-east Asia sent missionaries to the West, and one of the principal gifts they felt they had to share with war-torn Europe was Buddhist teaching about peace. There has also been a strong emphasis in Buddhism on sharing. The word for the Buddhist 'monk', *bhikkhu*, means 'one who shares', and the community life of the *bhikkhus,* supported by the wider lay community, has always been an important expression of Buddhist values. In various ways Buddhist ideas have begun to permeate Western culture, and some of the similarities between Buddhist and Christian ethical ideals have become better known in the West. Such qualities as compassion, humility, truth, and indiscriminate giving are emphasized in Buddhism as they are in Christian teaching. But attention has also been paid to differences. In a popular book of the nineteen-seventies, *Small is Beautiful*, E. F. Schumacher claimed that 'Buddhist economics' would pay particular attention to simplicity and non-violence, and so would be concerned to put people rather than just profits at the centre of economic decision-making, and would try not to consume non-renewable resources. The function of work in Buddhist understanding, claimed Schumacher, is 'to give a man a chance to utilise and develop his faculties; to enable him to overcome his ego-centredness by joining with other people in a common task; and to bring forth the goods and services needed for a becoming existence'.[13] It is also claimed by those with detailed knowledge of them that both Hinduism and Buddhism lead more naturally than does Christianity to the teaching of a reverence for all life in an environmentally friendly way.

In thinking about moral issues, however, it is important to recognize that religion plays only a limited part in the construction of ethical aims. Many other factors, including economic and political desires, play a large part in determining what a particular society will regard as good and desirable. One of the concerns of the religious believer should be to guard against the too easy adoption of religious sentiment by policy-makers to bolster economic or geopolitical ambitions. In such circumstances, religious believers must do all they can to avoid conflicts being presented as some kind of moral or even – God help us – religious crusade. In pursuing that modest aim, Christians may be fortified by the thought that the approach of Jesus of Nazareth to moral issues was not to lay down new commands but to question and tease out the meaning of existing ethical rules (chapter 4, p. 25). That approach should inform Christian ethics, whether the subject is as large-scale as war and peace or as intimate as sexual relationships. In choosing to sum up the ethical teaching of the *Torah* by quoting the two commandments to 'love the Lord your God' (Deuteronomy 6.5) and 'love your neighbour as yourself' (Leviticus 19.18) Jesus was pointing to guiding principles but refusing to spell out rules in detail.

There is much common ground on ethical matters between all the major religions. They all include moral teaching designed to mitigate the worst effects of self-centred and anti-social behaviour and to encourage values beneficial to the community as a whole. The moral, although sadly not always the doctrinal, teaching of all the great religions is concerned to weaken the hold of aggression, intolerance, and the irresponsible use of power, and to increase the practice of compassion, non-violence, and care for the weak and the oppressed.

Questions for discussion

1. Is it surprising that core ethical rules appear to be so similar in all the major religions?

2. How could 'Do not covet' be translated into guidelines for public morality today?

3. What does Jesus' use of Deuteronomy 6.5 and Leviticus 19.18 tell us about the application of ethical rules? How does that influence our interpretation of, say, the ten commandments?

13

Evangelism, Conversion, and Hospitality

Christianity is one of the world's great missionary religions. In common with Buddhism and Islam, Christianity has been strongly permeated by the conviction that it is the channel of a final truth which is of such importance that it must be made known to the whole of humankind. Buddhism was the first major missionary religion, and in its spread from India to south-east Asia and then northwards to China, Tibet, Korea and Japan it showed a remarkable ability to adapt to quite different cultural contexts. Although sometimes aided by the conversion of emperors or other rulers, it has been largely through the appeal of its teaching and the example of its practitioners that Buddhism has spread. Buddhist teachers and their converts in the West have said that it is more important that people heed the teaching of Buddhism than that they should be 'converted' and become paid-up Buddhists. The distinction is one we might bear in mind as we think about Christian evangelism.

The early spread of Christianity outside its original Jewish homeland, whilst less rapid than the spread of Islam 600 years or so later, was remarkable for the extent of its advance throughout the countries bordering the Mediterranean and on into Europe. And unlike Islam, which more often converted whole societies, Christian growth before the time of Constantine, in the fourth century, was usually the result of individual or small-group conversions. That early experience, brightly coloured by stories of martyrs and heroes of the faith and reinforced by New Testament teaching, has provided a basis for modern ideas about evangelism. We have noticed how certain Rebecca was of her church's duty to proclaim the gospel, and how she feared that might be compromised in inter-faith activities (chapter 1, pp. 5–7). John (chapter 3, pp. 15, 16) was moved by sermons on evangelism, and troubled by questions of how to translate the call to evangelize into the realities of his everyday life.

Evangelism has played a large part in Christian history, although the word itself is not found in the New Testament. It derives from the Greek *euangelion*, which is usually translated 'good news' or 'good tidings'. In modern Protestant use the word has assumed the sense of proclaiming the message of the gospel in speech or writing, although in a wider sense 'evangelism' includes the acting out of the values of the gospel in action. Certainly the history of Christian missions since the early nineteenth century includes many examples of evangelism being as much – sometimes more – concerned with such activities as medical work, education, and agricultural improvement as with preaching. And if a list were to be drawn up of modern 'heroes of the faith' it is likely that it would include rather more names of activists like Mother Teresa and Martin Luther King Jr than it would the names of preachers. We noticed that in the work of the Christian charity the question arose of whether the faith of the workers should be made explicit or whether the work itself should be seen as sufficient expression of Christian faith (chapter 5, pp. 26, 27). That, too, expresses a tension already evident in New Testament times, as we see in the question posed by the Letter of James: 'What good is it, my friends, for someone to say he has faith when his actions do nothing to show it?' (James 2.14). And that in turn reinforces much of the teaching of Jesus, with its concern for the practical application of faith and its impatience with hair-splitting theological arguments.

On their long country walk John and Ted discussed evangelism, and wondered where to draw the line between evangelism and proselytizing. They concluded that there might be a distinction between an evangelism in which the Christian tries to share the treasures of his faith with others and the proselytizing which aims to increase the influence of one's own group or community (chapter 3, p. 18). In matters of inter-faith

77

relationships, that is a distinction of crucial importance. Some religious teaching places great emphasis on the importance of disinterested action. That does not mean acting without interest or a sense of involvement; it does mean doing things because they are the right things to do, rather than because they bring an immediate reward or are to our own benefit. There is an admirable integrity in acts which are done simply out of moral conviction and without any regard for whether or not they bring praise – or blame – to us. We notice in the Gospels how such an attitude is commended in parable (The Good Samaritan, Luke 10.25–37) and in the activity of Jesus. Robert mentioned to Rebecca (chapter 1, p. 7) the incident of the healing of the centurion's son (Matthew 8.5–13), in which story there is no indication that Jesus expected to gain a convert from the man he so much admired. As the story is recorded there, it is an example of disinterested action.

That is the kind of integrity we might look for, especially in relationships with people of other faiths. If we want to get to know them or to understand their traditions simply in order to win them to our way of believing, we can hardly be regarded as acting with integrity. But if we approach them from the security of our own faith and with a desire to share the treasures of our faith with them, while we also hear about the treasures of their faith, we shall be acting with integrity and in a spirit of Christian love. If our concern in meeting and sharing with people of other faiths is that in us as well as in them there may be 'the increase of the Christlike person' (chapter 10, p. 62), then we shall be approaching dialogue in the right spirit. The richly talented Catholic scholar and writer, William Johnston, suggested that in dialogue we preach the gospel because we love the gospel and want to share its treasures with those we love. But in doing that, we avoid any undue pressure: 'No beguiling promises. No stern threats. No charming enticements.' It is then up to the other person to accept what they want to accept. Any conversion or change of faith is not in our hands; it is the work of God, and 'we never break into the inner sanctum of conscience where the human person is alone with God'.[14] Proclaiming the gospel may be done more effectively in deeds than in words. Actions, commitment to justice and peace, and a loving concern for other people are likely to be more impressive than words alone. But when the gospel is presented in words, it can still be done in a disinterested way, acknowledging that those to whom we speak will make their own responses in their own ways. True evangelism must be based upon the appeal of the gospel message; but it will be an open appeal. Most Christians today recognize and guard the right of people to accept or reject what is offered, and to change their minds about their religious allegiance if that is what they wish.

Evangelism also recognizes the boundaries of different faith groups, and the difficulties of crossing them. The great religions of the world are not simply about private belief; they also have to do with culture, and histories and social contexts from which one can extricate oneself only with great difficulty. In practice people cannot simply pick and choose from a whole galaxy of faiths. Religions require commitment of their followers, and so do not readily encourage syncretism – a mix of religious ideas and practices selected from the world's religions as a bag of sweets may be filled from the shelves. Recognizing that, the followers of one faith talking to the followers of another may at the same time both accept and reject the possibility of conversion. So John and Ted concluded that it would be unwise for the loyal and practising member of one faith group to move to another faith group. But they might also have recognized that in any true dialogue there is likely to be a kind of conversion, as people revise and re-think their understanding of their own faith in the light of someone else's beliefs and practice. And that would be significant for dialogue. The point of listening as well as speaking, of approaching other people with disinterested love, is not only that in such a way is integrity shown, but also that in dialogue religions can deepen and purify themselves.[15] As individuals, we see our own faults and perhaps our own special talents more clearly when they are viewed in the light of the gifts and experiences of others. So in religious encounter, we understand our own faith more clearly, and become better equipped to reform it where it is in need of change, when we meet and understand those of other faiths.

Such attitudes also make it easier to regard hospitality as a corollary rather than a contradiction of evangelism. It is difficult to practise genuine hospitality if, as soon as our neighbour comes into our house, we give the impression that most of all we want to tell her that she is wrong, and that what we then want is to make her just like us. Equally, we shall quickly cross from evangelism into the dangerous and unpleasant area of proselytizing if our main motive in inviting and meeting people of other faiths in a church setting is to increase the number of our members or the importance of our church. When Robert drove across town to a venue that was strange to him, he was impressed by the hospitality offered at the Sikh gurdwara (chapter 1, p. 3). Might we learn something from that?

Other Christian visitors will also find a warm welcome at Sikh places of worship and community activities. There will often be a community room or hall, open most of the day, where people gather to meet and chat. Elderly Sikh men may be reading Punjabi newspapers. Coffee will be available, and possibly a meal served at lunchtime, and the visitor is likely to be offered either or both. Early in Sikh history the practice of offering food to all, served in the same place and prepared in the same kitchen, was a symbol of the Sikh refusal to allow a religious significance to caste. Nowadays it is much more a sign of the hospitality and tolerance which Sikhs will regard as hallmarks of their faith. If the visitor goes on from community hall to the worship room of the gurdwara the same sense of hospitality may be evident, although in different ways.

Provided she observes the usual courtesies of removing her shoes and covering her head, she will be able to sit and observe or join in the worship. When *prasad* is passed around (chapter 7, p. 41) it will be offered to the visitor. And it is very likely that someone will speak to her, enquire about her own religious beliefs, and perhaps quote some words of Guru Nanak to the effect that, 'There is but one Giver of all life, let me never forget him.'[16]

Hospitality is indeed a tangible part of the life of most gurdwaras to be found in Britain. It is to be hoped that the same is true of Christian churches. Newcomers will be welcomed, invited to join the worship, and asked for their names and addresses. The question of hospitality, however, takes us beyond those formalities. It leads to further questions, such as: 'Is the welcome an act of disinterested concern, or is it given in the hope that the visitor will become part of the congregation. If it is evident that such will not be the case, is the welcome still as warm?' Hospitality, if it is genuine, must include tolerance. How do churches appear on a measure of tolerance, I wonder? It is not particularly easy to find passages of scripture or even hymns that will reinforce tolerance as the subject of a service. Many passages, even from the New Testament, speak louder of intolerance. Yet the Jesus of the Gospels is a more tolerant figure than is sometimes thought. His disciples were once asked: 'Why is it that your teacher eats with tax collectors and sinners?' His splendid reply was: 'It is not the healthy who need a doctor, but the sick. Go and learn what this text means. "I require mercy, not sacrifice"' (Matthew 9.11–13). Hospitality, tolerance, disinterested love, and care for people regardless of who they are or of what religious persuasion they may be, are among the very best of the consequences of a Christian faith. How wonderful then that such qualities are not threatened, but can be enhanced, by encounters with people of other faiths.

Questions for discussion

1. How would you distinguish between evangelism and proselytizing? Make a list of activities which could be included under each title.

2. Would you think it legitimate to seek converts from (a) members of other denominations; (b) members of other faiths; (c) only from those with no religious faith?

3. Work out an act of worship focussed on the subject of 'tolerance', and then consider whether members of your church would regard what you have produced as properly 'Christian'?

Part 3

People of Other Faiths in Britain

14

Jews

The history of the Jews in Britain is a complex story of acceptance and rejection. Jews were present in England in the mediaeval period, and from the time of the Norman conquest they performed an essential commercial role in the English economy. Their fortunes changed when the fervour stirred up by the Crusades – attempting to persuade people to travel to Palestine to fight the 'infidel' Muslims – drew attention to the Jews, who could also be regarded as 'infidels' but who were conveniently closer at hand. The massacre of Jews at York in 1190 was one example of the anti-Jewish feeling of this period, which culminated in the expulsion of Jews from England in 1290 by order of King Edward I.

No Jews were legally allowed in the territory ruled by the English sovereign from 1290 until the time of the Civil War. In 1656 Oliver Cromwell's Council of State declared that the presence of Jews in the country could be regarded as legitimate. It was mostly Sephardic Jews (whose origins lay in Palestine and Spain, but who came to Britain from the Netherlands) who formed the basis of a small but increasingly influential and prosperous Jewish community which fitted easily into British society. In the last two decades of the nineteenth century that situation changed when a wave of persecution (known as 'pogroms') broke out in Russia and Poland, then the home of many Ashkenazim Jews. The Ashkenazim were Jews of central Europe who spoke Yiddish (a mixture of German and Hebrew) and whose Jewishness was clearly visible in dress and custom – partly as a result of having been compelled on many occasions to live in ghettos. Refugees fleeing from the persecution in eastern Europe moved westwards, many of them hoping to reach the United States of America. Some achieved that goal, thus forming the basis of the large Jewish communities of north America; others arrived in Britain, settling in the east end of

London, as well as in Manchester, Leeds and parts of the north-east.

Many of the Jewish immigrants set up in trade on their own account, particularly in tailoring, cigar-making, and shoe-making. These were trades that could be pursued independently of the willingness of the host society to employ them, and enabled them to work in family units. They were, however, subject to much criticism and prejudice, and politicians in areas where the immigrants settled were quick to take advantage of that. The Jewish newcomers were accused of taking people's jobs and housing, of being unhygienic, of having different customs, of not speaking English, of being lazy and of working too hard. They were in fact subject to all the accusations later levelled against immigrants from the New Commonwealth. In 1902 a Royal Commission on Alien Immigration was set up to consider the charges being made against Jewish immigrants; the Commission found that hardly any of the charges were true, but nonetheless an Aliens Act was passed in 1905 to restrict the numbers allowed to enter the country.

The arrival of the Ashkenazim led to a larger and different kind of Jewish presence in Britain, but numbers were still small. By 1911 it was estimated that there were about 300,000 Jews in Britain, and in spite of many changes it is probable that the number of practising Jews is still around that level. But the Jews have come to be regarded as a model of successful accommodation on the part of immigrants to a host society. There was considerable movement from the original areas of settlement (from the East End to Golders Green or Hove, for example); many Jews were very successful in different spheres of British life and in course of time most Jews became indistinguishable on limited acquaintance from any other British citizens. Of course, there have been subsequent arrivals and departures among the Jewish community. During the 1930s Jews from Germany and German-occupied Europe sought refuge from persecution in Britain, as elsewhere. And with the founding of the State of Israel in 1948, Jews from Britain were among those who migrated to the new nation which is so important to most Jews, whether religious or secular.

Jewish religious practice in Britain reflects developments which have taken place over many centuries. A mistake Christians sometimes make is to regard Judaism as essentially 'the religion of the Old Testament'. Although there is continuity between the Hebrew Bible and Jewish practice today, there have been many fundamental changes since that time. The constituent elements of the Hebrew scriptures – *Torah*, or the first five books of the Bible, prophets, psalms, and wisdom writings – remain extremely important in Jewish life and worship. But the development of the *Mishnah* and the *Talmud* during the first few centuries of the Common Era endowed Judaism with a vast amount of authoritative material which provides additional guidance in the interpretation of Jewish traditions.

In the modern period different kinds of Judaism have developed, partly in response to the post-enlightenment influences which have so affected the understanding of texts and traditions in religions generally. Orthodox Judaism adheres to the view that Jewish law, or *Torah,* as well as a set of oral traditions which enable the *Torah* to be interpreted (and which came to be incorporated in the *Mishnah* and *Talmud*) are the result of a revelation given to Moses at Sinai, and so are a kind of divine knowledge, valid for all time. This kind of understanding is regarded by the Orthodox as a defence of true Jewish faith against the inroads of modern cultural influences. The modern Orthodox movement developed in Hungary and Germany in the nineteenth century, and is now most strongly represented in the USA and in Israel. But Orthodox Jews also constitute a majority of practising Jews in the UK, and the Chief Rabbi is drawn from their ranks.

Reform Jews, also known as Liberal or Progressive, take a different view of revelation and tradition. They accept the value and use of historical and biblical criticism, and so do not regard the written or oral laws as necessarily constituting a literal record of what was revealed to Moses. Reform movements have commonly held to a view of progressive revelation; the view that is, that with the progress of knowledge there is a gradual deepening of understanding of what it is that lies behind the texts. Differences between Orthodox and Liberal or Progressive Jews are very evident to the Christian visitor to a synagogue, not least because Orthodox worship is normally conducted in Hebrew whilst English is used for much of the worship of Reformed synagogues.

Of 300,000 Jews in the UK today, the Board of Deputies of British Jews estimates that there are about 200,000 Jews involved with synagogues. Of those, two-thirds are in the 'United Synagogue' (Orthodox), and one-third in the Reform (Liberal and Progressive) movement. However, membership of the United Synagogue is currently declining, while synagogues of the Reformed traditions remain fairly stable in their membership. The family has always been of great importance in Jewish life and worship – the celebration of Sabbath and of festivals in the home is arguably more important than what happens in the synagogue. Because of that, the role of the Jewish wife and mother has always been very significant in religious terms, and one of the common definitions of a Jew is somebody who has a Jewish mother. One of the great concerns of Jewish leaders in the UK today is with an increasing tendency for Jews to 'marry out', and so to weaken traditional Jewish practices and lessen the number of practising Jews.

15

Muslims

We tend to think of Islam, the religion of the Muslims, as chronologically the last of the three great Middle Eastern religions. Islamic worship and scriptures use the language of Arabic; Muhammad, the great prophet of Islam, was an Arabic speaker, and Islam arose in the desert cities of Arabia. But in the modern world a majority of Muslims live south and east of Karachi, and in that sense Islam is very much an Asian religion. Today, more than seven million Muslims live in Europe, and so perhaps we had better not categorize Islam as belonging to this or that part of the world, but simply acknowledge that it is one of the great world faiths.

Certainly it is from the Indian sub-continent, from Pakistan and Bangladesh, that most Muslim families in Britain have come. In 1947, when the former British India and the Indian States attained independence, the area was partitioned into India and Pakistan. India, predominantly Hindu but with a substantial eleven per cent Muslim minority, chose to construct a secular constitution which gave no advantage to members of any one religion. The leaders of Pakistan, on the other hand, having campaigned for Pakistan as a separate homeland for Muslims, framed an Islamic constitution for their country. Originally, Pakistan consisted of two wings: West Pakistan on the north-western borders of India, and East Pakistan set between Bengal and Assam in the north-east. In 1971 a civil war resulted in the creation of Bangladesh as a new nation in place of the former East Pakistan. Most Pakistanis – in the north-west – speak Urdu, a mixture of Persian and Hindi, whilst the majority language of Bangladesh is Bengali.

One of the striking things about migration from Pakistan and Bangladesh to Britain from the 1950s onwards, is how restricted and localized are the places from which people have come. There are a number of towns and villages in the western part of Pakistan, near the borders with the Indian Punjab – Mirpur, Lyallpur, etc. – from which Pakistani immigrants came, whilst a large majority of immigrants from Bangladesh came from the area around Sylhet, which at one time provided crew members for British ships sailing out of Calcutta. Areas of settlement in this country have also been remarkably concentrated – Sylhettis in the east end of London, in the very streets occupied by Jews at the beginning of the century; Mirpuris and Punjabis in Rochdale, where in the late 1970s over 100 families in the Wardleworth area of the town had come from Mirpur and 200 families in the Tweedale Street area were from the Pakistani Punjab.[17]

The great majority of those who came from Pakistan and Bangladesh were practising Muslims, often from rural areas where attitudes to religion and morality were still very conservative. Studies undertaken in the 1970s and 1980s showed how strange and disturbing some aspects of British life seemed to the newcomers, especially when they had little experience of knowing members of the host community well and when perceptions were often read from television screens (chapter 4, pp. 23, 24). But the close-knit Muslim communities provided much support. Although Pakistani Muslims do not share the caste-system of Hindus, they do have a kinship system, known as *bhiraderi*, which creates mutual obligations between members of the same extended family and sometimes between different families. *Bhiraderi* has been important among new immigrants in determining such things as choice of residence, job selection, and reciprocal services. Incidentally, people are not always aware that in a wider sense the giving of a gift to a member of an Asian family often results in a gift being given in return; to refuse such a gift, perhaps out of a mistaken sense of kindness, would be to cause offence. The giving and receiving of gifts establishes mutual obligations.

Bhiraderi is a cultural rather than a religious custom, and it is not always easy to distinguish between those two things. But

Islam as a faith and a way of life is of very great importance to many of those whose origins lie in Pakistan and Bangladesh. There is an essential simplicity to Islamic practice which makes it possible for anyone to follow the faith. Essential to being a Muslim is submission (the name of the religion – Islam – means 'submission') to the will of God. Islam is much more concerned with doing the will of God than with somehow 'knowing' God, or entering into a relationship with God. And there are clear guidelines as to what has to be done. A fundamental requirement is acceptance and recitation of the *shahada*, the statement of faith that 'There is no God but God, and Muhammad is his messenger'. The words are normally said in Arabic, in which language the word for God is Allah. Additionally, the Muslim is expected to accept the other four basic duties which together with the *shahada* make up the 'Five Pillars of Islam'. They are: the set prayers, said five times a day; almsgiving; fasting, especially during the month of Ramadan; and, where possible, pilgrimage to Mecca at least once in a lifetime. Additionally, the Muslim life is defined and informed by the teaching of the scriptures, the *Qur'an*, which according to Islam was revealed in Arabic to the prophet Muhammad, and the sacred law, or *Shari'a*. Right conduct is of central importance in Islamic life.

Muslim prayer may be said anywhere, but the hours of prayer will be observed in most mosques, and some will avail themselves of the opportunity of joining other Muslims there. On Fridays there is special observance at the mosque, normally between noon and 3.0 p.m., with prayers and often an address. There are now more than a thousand mosques in Britain, the majority of which are in adapted buildings. The purpose-built mosques are often architecturally striking, with a clarity of line and a simplicity of interior. Human and animal figures are deliberately avoided in the decoration of mosques, for fear that simple worshippers may associate such figures with God. But decoration with geometrical designs and arabesque writing (that is, verses from the *Qur'an* in Arabic script) provide beautiful and striking designs. The two commonest words in mosque calligraphy are Allah and Muhammad. Mosques do not normally provide seating; worshippers stand, moving and prostrating themselves in rhythm to the prayers, or sit on the floor during the address or in private worship.

Although Muslims often emphasize the essential unity of all Muslims, there are different strands in Islam, of which the most notable are *Sunni* and *Shi'ah*. The *Sunni*, who constitute the greatest number of Muslims, regard themselves as the representatives of mainstream and orthodox Islam. The *Shi'ah*, found particularly in Iran and Iraq, but also in Pakistan, Bangladesh and India, developed after a dispute which arose some thirty years after the death of Muhammad, in the seventh century CE, over the question of who should be the successors of Muhammad as Caliph. The *Shi'ites* believed that Caliphs should be in the line of succession of Muhammad's cousin and son-in-law, 'Ali ibn Abi Talib. The Ismailis, a liberal and westernized community, developed from within the *Shi'ah* tradition.

In Britain, there are other groupings of Muslims which impinge more directly on the lives of ordinary Muslims. Among the most significant of these are the *Deobandi* and the *Barelvi*, both of which are *Sunni* sub-groups or schools, with their own mosques and organizations. Both developed, albeit in quite different ways, in nineteenth-century India; there continue to be disagreements between the two groups. The *Barelvi* developed in opposition to modernization, and incorporated into their practices many local customs of nineteenth-century India. They accord a very high sacred status to the prophet Muhammad, and even suggest that Muhammad can intercede for people with God. *Barelvis*, whose mosques are very common in the UK, played a major role in agitation against Salman Rushdie's *Satanic Verses*. The *Deobandis* originally attempted to accommodate Muslim practices with their situation in a colonial nation. They were particularly concerned with the question of how they could live as Muslims in a non-Islamic State, and their answer was to limit their relationships with the State as far as possible. They were anxious to avoid the surrounding influences of Hindus and even of *Shi'ite* Muslims.

One of the features of local mosques in Britain is that many serve Muslim communities drawn from particular parts of the world and particular language areas, and because of that distinctions between different mosques in large towns and cities often have to do with the different ethnic origins of the worshippers. Some centrally located mosques, however, do serve disparate Muslim communities. The splendid Regent's Park Mosque in London, for example, provides a focus for Islamic life in the capital, has a management committee which includes representatives of all the Islamic nations whose ambassadors or High Commissioners are accredited to the UK, and serves a wide and diverse Muslim community, including many visitors to London. In recent years British Muslims have been concerned to find ways of focussing their concerns and finding a common voice on public issues. One means to that end was the creation of the British Council of Mosques.

Muslims, in common with other religious believers in Britain, have their worries about the allegiance of younger generations. In some cases, in the face of perceived – and often real – prejudice against Islam, young Muslims show considerable zeal in the protection of their faith. But there are also undoubtedly many cases in which younger people who have been influenced by Western ideas find family traditions and expectations difficult to accommodate. One of the big issues for Muslims is education: should there be State-funded Muslim schools which could provide an Islamic education and inculcate Islamic values among those growing up in a society which is often perceived to be antipathetic both to Islam and to religion in general?

In recent years the dangers of people in the West caricaturing, or even demonizing, Islam has become acute. Some commentators suggest that the fall of 'the evil empire' of communism has left a void which Westerners have a psychological need to fill. Edward Said claimed that what he termed the 'Western Orientalist' view of Islam rested upon feelings of cultural and intellectual superiority and created a fear of Islamic political and military resurgence, leading to even narrower stereotyping of Islam. Recent excesses of Islamic fundamentalists in Iran and elsewhere may well have enhanced this view. No doubt Christians will wish to resist such crude stereotyping and acknowledge the variety and richness of Islamic traditions.

16

Hindus

Hindus are among the most open and tolerant of religious believers to be found in the UK. Their traditions are many and diverse, and the varieties of practices and beliefs that historically have constituted Hinduism encourage the view that there is likely to be truth in all religion. It is difficult to estimate the number of practising Hindus in Britain. The 1991 'Social Trends' report gave a figure of 1,323,000 for all British Asians permanently resident in the UK; of those 787,000 were of Indian background (and so mostly Hindus and Sikhs in religion); 485,000 were under 16, and mostly born in the UK. Perhaps a figure of around 400,000 for those who would identify themselves as 'Hindus' when asked to state their religion (on entering hospital, for example) may be about right.

There have been Hindus visiting Britain and living in Britain for a very long time. Although few in number, Hindus were to be found in Britain in the eighteenth and nineteenth centuries, and some notable Hindus, including Nehru and Gandhi, studied in Britain during the period of the British Raj. Most Hindus found in Britain today, however, are from families which arrived in a two-pronged migration spanning the years from the mid 1950s to the early 1970s. Many of the first arrivals were from the Indian Punjab and from Gujarat, which had a long history of migration to eastern and southern Africa. To those earlier arrivals were added the considerable number of Hindus who came from East Africa, leaving Kenya during a period of Africanization in the late 1960s and being expelled from Uganda by Idi Amin in 1972. Today the majority of Hindus in Britain are from a Gujarati background, although a large number of both Gujarati and Punjabi families came to the UK. from East Africa; it is not at all unusual to come across practising Hindus who came to Britain as immigrants but who have never been to India.

The term 'Hinduism' can be confusing. It was applied to the religion of Hindus by Europeans who seem to have assumed that any religion must be an 'ism' – a more or less consistent ideology. This is unlikely to be true of any religion, but it is even less true of Hinduism than of most others. The term cannot be avoided, of course, and has now passed into common use, by Hindus and non-Hindus alike. In fact, the word Hinduism refers to a variety of practices and beliefs which arose and flourished on the Indian sub-continent from probably as early as 2,500 BCE, producing profound philosophy, carefully thought-out spiritual practices, and exuberant worship. But Hinduism cannot neatly be defined in terms of a founder or a creed – the religion has neither. One common feature of Hinduism historically has been a remarkably strong system of social control: every Hindu has been born into a community, known as *jati* (birth) which in turn can be related to a notional grading of society into four main groups (*varna*). *Jati* is the essence of the caste system, which has persisted with remarkable strength for nearly three thousand years but which in the modern world is undergoing many changes.

Traditionally, worship for Hindus has been carried out in the home, with family or private prayer, but with social events centred upon the many festivals. Visits to the temples (which vary from small shrines to vast complexes) have always been regarded as entirely optional activities for Hindus in India, and even there worship has normally been the private acts of individuals rather than congregational worship. But Indian temples have provided a focus for pilgrimage, which has been of great importance, and for the discussions of scholars and the dissemination of the teaching of different schools of thought.

Most Hindus will say that they believe in one God who is manifested in various forms. So the many gods whose images may be seen in temples (Krishna, Rama, Durga, Ganesh) are understood to be manifestations of the one Supreme Reality. The belief in an ultimate reality (sometimes termed *brahman*) which can be encountered in personal experience and is revealed in a series of incarnations unites Hindus and provides for sophisticated understandings of God as well as simple devotion to a personal God. That is one of the things that binds Hindus together, in spite of regional and other differences. Other common beliefs include *karma,* the idea that every action – and thought – produces a consequence which then has to be worked out, either in this life or in a subsequent existence. A complementary belief, held by many Hindus, is reincarnation, and the idea that one's behaviour in this life (or *karma*) conditions the nature of rebirth has been widely held. Another related belief is in *dharma,* a word that can mean a universal sense of right and wrong, or the law of conduct applicable to individuals and dependent upon their role and position in society. It also has the meaning of personal obligation derived from Hindu religious and moral teaching. So a Hindu might respond to thanks for some service done with the disarming comment: 'It is my *dharma*'.

There is more than one goal of life in Hindu as in other religious practices. Many will be concerned day by day with pragmatic goals which have to do with healing, for example, and so prayers will be addressed to God or the gods for health or for other benefits. Slightly more distant is the dharmik goal of a better rebirth in another life. And finally (although all three may be held together in closer or more remote focus) is the goal of liberation or salvation (*moksha*). Some Hindus will interpret *moksha* as liberation from the round of birth and rebirth; for others, *moksha* will mean salvation as deliverance by and communion with God.

Whilst Hinduism may appear to be complicated, with so many layers of traditions and development, there is at its heart an essential simplicity which naturally assumes dependence upon God or the divine, sees no separation between the sacred and the profane, and admires austere living on the part of those who profess religious belief.

Regional differences in practices, festivals, caste groups and even deities are a feature of Hinduism in India, and inevitably an element of that is found in the British Hindu experience. The predominance of Gujarati or Punjabi backgrounds (whether directly or via East Africa) is reflected in names, favourite festivals, food and in other ways. For example, the largest Hindu community in Britain is that of Gujarati Patidars (one of whose common names is Patel), and Patidar values, business skills, and financial acumen are therefore commonly associated with British Hindus generally. But many things about culture and religion change when people migrate across great distances, and Hinduism in Britain is in the process of significant changes. Caste in the traditional form in which it functioned in village India (the physical separation of castes, jobs determined by caste) does not survive in Britain – or for that matter in modern urban India. Because of this, many Hindus will say that caste is no longer practised in Britain, meaning perhaps that it does not retain its religious significance. But caste remains important for mutual assistance, in financial and other ways, as well as in marriage and social life.

In temples there is sometimes a deliberate attempt to cater for a variety of Indian backgrounds, and that may be reflected in more eclectic worship and festivals than would be found in a temple serving a single community. On the other hand, there are temples which revolve around the teaching and inspiration of a particular person (at the Radha-Krishna Temple in Balham a remarkable woman known as Mother Shyama is the focus of the temple's life), or serve a clearly defined and restricted community (as does the temple of the Caribbean Hindu Society in Brixton).[18] But there are signs of particular developments taking place in British temples. One is an increasing use of congregational worship, which would be unusual in an Indian Hindu temple. Another is the gradual construction of a common view of what it is that constitutes Hindu belief, partly in response to the need of temple staff to explain themselves to visitors, in a way that would not be thought necessary in India. The National Council of Hindu Temples provides the opportunity for British Hindus to speak with a common voice, something that Hindus in India are not able to do. There are other Hindu organizations in Britain, including the Vishwa Hindu Parishad, in Croydon, which aims to establish networks among Hindus who have come to the UK from India. The Arya Pratinidhi Sabha continues the traditions and teachings of the Arya Samaj, a nineteenth-century Hindu reform movement which has been concerned not only to reform but also to defend Hindus against criticism and attempts at conversion.

Also important for many British Hindus is the Swaminarayan movement, which developed in the Gujarat area of India in the late nineteenth century and has since spread along the routes of the Hindu diaspora. The movement attracts recruits from a wide range of Hindus, rather than being simply regional or community based, and is well organized and supported. The Shri Swaminarayan Mandir, opened in north London in 1995, is a most impressive example of a large Hindu temple-complex. In addition to the worship area of the temple, there is a prayer hall to accommodate 2,500 people, a 'cultural complex', and a permanent exhibition on 'Understanding Hinduism'. The Mandir was described by one British national newspaper as the 'most remarkable London monument of the late 20th century'.

Another new Hindu movement visible in Britain is ISKCON, the International Society for Krishna Consciousness, better known as the Hare Krishna movement. Founded in New York in 1966 by Swami Bhaktivedanta Prabhupadi, the Society has its UK headquarters at Bhaktivedanta Manor, in Hertfordshire. ISKCON has recruited widely among non-Hindus, and has been publicly visible through the chanting and singing of its saffron-clad devotees on the streets of British cities. The movement reflects the practices of Hindu *bhakti*, or devotional, schools, and particularly emphasizes the chanting of the name of Krishna, made popular by Sri Chaitanya, a notable Bengali religious leader of the sixteenth century.

17

Jains

The Jains, or Jainas, are a small community in Britain, but their temples in London and Leicester attract many visitors and their teaching and life-style provide an interesting study in similarity and contrast with that of Hindus. There are said to be about six million Jains world-wide, mostly in India, where their chief centres of influence are in Gujarat and Rajasthan. Jainism developed in India between the eighth and sixth centuries BCE. The word Jain is derived from the root *ji* which means 'to conquer', and in its early developments the Jains were particularly concerned with the conquest of the body by the spirit. There is a strong emphasis in Jainism on *karma*, and the cycle of birth and rebirth. The goal of the believer is to break that cycle and so to attain liberation. In order to avoid bad *karma* and develop good *karma* Jainism has always emphasized the importance of right conduct. In that connection it introduced teaching centred around the five ethical precepts of non-violence, celibacy (complete celibacy for monks, and sex only within marriage for lay followers), truthfulness, not stealing, and not coveting. Non-violence is an especially important part of Jain teaching, and that is applied in relationships with people and animals, and also demands that Jains be strict vegetarians.

Commitment to non-violence has influenced the type of lay occupations open to Jains. Traditionally, they have been traders and merchants in textiles and jewellery, and financiers; more recently, Jains have entered medicine and the technical industries. The principal of reverence for life which is so central to Jainism also encourages interest in environmental concerns.

Jains revere a group of twenty-four *Tirthankaras* (literally, 'ford-crossers'), who are believed to have attained liberation and so crossed from the material to the spiritual world. These emancipated beings are believed to be able to help others on their spiritual quest. Theoretically, Jains do not subscribe to the worship of God or the gods, although in practice there are various gods and goddesses who are accommodated into the system of belief as helpers of the Jinas (the 'conquerors' or *Tirthankaras*) but who lack the ability to assist in the all-important quest for liberation. Images of the deities, of the ascetic Jinas seated in yogic posture, and elaborate paintings of the cosmic and mortal realms form the subjects of highly developed Jain art. Between November 1995 and February 1996 the Victoria and Albert Museum staged a major exhibition of 'Jain Art from India'.

There are about 30,000 Jains in Britain today, most of whom were part of the migration from East Africa in the late 1960s and early 1970s. The temple in Leicester is the largest outside India, and the first traditional Jain temple in the West. The complex of the Leicester Jain Centre includes a museum and a Jain Academy, established in association with courses in Jain studies at the De Montfort University.

18

Sikhs

Sikhs are an important and visible part of the British religious landscape. By comparison with the major world faiths the religion of the Sikhs is relatively new and culturally homogeneous. Sikhism developed in the Punjab, in the north-west of India, between the end of the fifteenth and the late seventeenth centuries CE, and retains a Punjabi cultural and linguistic background. In present-day India, the Sikhs constitute about two per cent of the total population – it is often a surprise to people to learn that there are fewer Sikhs than Christians in India. Sikhs have always been a vigorous and adventurous people, and from the Punjab they have migrated to the cities of India and to many other parts of the world.

Sikhism began with the teaching of Guru Nanak, a teacher and inspirational figure who bore some resemblance to leaders of north Indian *bhakti* movements. Nanak used both Hindu and Muslim names for God, and attracted followers from both the major religions. He taught that there is only one God, whom he described as the 'true creator', formless, with no intermediaries – so he discounted Hindu practices related to images and Hindu teaching about *avatars*, or incarnations, of God. He did accept *karma* and belief in rebirth. At his death Guru Nanak named a successor to lead the Sikhs (the word derives from one which means 'follower' or 'disciple'), and during the following two hundred years ten Gurus, from Guru Nanak to Guru Gobind Singh, led the Sikh community and established it as a separate and clearly defined religion. Shortly before his death, Guru Gobind Singh established the *Khalsa*, the community of initiated Sikhs who were bidden to reject discrimination on the grounds of caste, to shun superstition and idolatry, and to believe in the one true God. Those who became *Khalsa* Sikhs accepted the wearing of five visible signs of their commitment, including uncut hair (hence the turban), a steel bracelet (a reminder of the unity of God), and a small dagger, a symbol of resistance to evil. Guru Gobind Singh also announced the end of the succession of Gurus, and declared that henceforth the Sikh scriptures, the *Adi Granth*, or *Guru Granth Sahib* (containing the teaching of Guru Nanak and some of the other Gurus) would become the spiritual guide of the Sikh community.

During their early history the Sikhs often suffered persecution from the Muslim rulers of northern India, and the visible signs were one indication of their determination to stand up against oppression. Sikhs acquired a not entirely undeserved reputation as a martial people, a distinction which was enhanced when, after the Indian revolt of 1857, the British rulers of India made a special point of recruiting Sikhs to the army. Sikh experience in the armed forces in the twentieth century was one of the factors that encouraged many of them to migrate to areas they had visited in the course of their life in the services.

A number of Sikhs arrived in Britain in the 1930s, but it was in the early 1950s that the migration of Sikh men from the Punjab began. The early arrivals made strenuous efforts to fit in to British society, often shaving off beards and cutting their hair in the forlorn hope that in this way they would become more acceptable. The cultural patterns of Sikh life in Britain changed when, in anticipation of the 1962 Commonwealth Immigration Act, wives and children came to join the male immigrants. The establishment of Sikh families encouraged a renewal of Sikh religious life. In the period up to 1959 only seven new Sikh gurdwaras (or temples) had been established in Britain, in the following fifteen years nearly fifty gurdwaras were established (chapter 13, pp. 80, 81). In the new climate, many men renewed their *Khalsa* vows, and attendance at gurdwara, the wearing of turbans, and other visible signs of Sikh commitment were adopted with pride. Substantial Sikh communities developed in Gravesend, Bedford, Leeds, and Southall.[19] A further development in Sikh settlement in Britain followed the expulsion of British Asians from Uganda in 1972.

Although Sikhs have always insisted that caste has no religious significance for them – and this was one distinction between Sikhs and Hindus – the all-embracing social practice of caste was something they could not escape. In the Punjab the Jats, a caste of farmers and landowners, were regarded as socially superior and tended to have the greatest influence in religious affairs. The Ramgarhias, originally a community of artisans, had a lower status in the Punjab. It was largely Jats who came to Britain directly from the Punjab, and Ramgarhias who migrated first to East Africa and then to Britain. In East Africa the Ramgarhias had become prosperous, and they had acquired skills in urban societies that helped them settle quickly in Britain; they had also developed fairly conservative attitudes to their religion and to marriage and other social customs in East Africa.[20] In Britain it soon became obvious that the position of Jats and Ramgarhias had been reversed, with the Ramgarhias the more prosperous community. In some towns and cities there are separate gurdwaras for Jats and Ramgarhias, and in such cases different attitudes to Indian politics may also be evident, with Jats from the Punjab much more likely to be interested in Punjabi politics than the Ramgarhias, whose connection with such things is much more distant.

To point out that different communities of Sikhs do things differently is not to be unduly critical of Sikhs. It is rather to point out that differences within major religious or ethnic groups are as important as the differences between various kinds of Christians. Parminder Bhachu pointed out in the conclusion to her interesting study of East African Sikhs in Britain in the 1980s that the situation and cultural patterns of minorities are much more fluid and complex than normally assumed by the host community.[21]

Sikhs in Britain are generally tolerant of people of other faiths, welcoming to those who visit their gurdwaras, and conscious of the fact that their own religious tradition began with teaching which sought to identify the essentials of spiritual and moral life among the prevailing faiths in the Punjab.

19

Buddhists

The presence of Buddhists in Britain is not the result of migration. Most British Buddhists are converts who have moved from a Christian or secular-humanist background to become Buddhists. The appeal of Buddhism in the West is an interesting, and for Christians, an instructive example of the need felt by many people for religious practices, a moral framework and a path to follow without the attendant problems of belief in the supernatural or in an interventionist God.

As a missionary religion (chapter 12, p. 76), Buddhism spread from India to many parts of South East Asia and then northwards to China, Tibet, Korea and Japan. The movement began with the teaching and experience of Siddhartha, the Buddha, who lived in the late sixth and early fifth centuries. The Buddha is regarded as a great teacher who achieved enlightenment and then taught the truth of the Middle Way – avoiding excesses of extreme asceticism on the one hand and indulgence on the other. Central to his teaching is the recognition that everything is impermanent. The world and everything in it is constantly changing, developing, growing, decaying, dying. At any one moment that change is hard to recognize: people perceive the world around them as constant and stable. But that is not the case. Possessions, relationships, youth, beauty – all will disappear. Life is therefore unsatisfactory (the Buddha used the word *dukkha,* from his own north Indian language of Pali, for this state of impermanence and unsatisfactoriness).

The early Buddhist teaching appears to have been concerned with this insight into the human condition rather than with the conventional religious teaching of the day. Indeed, Buddhism has been presented as a kind of revolt against the prevailing Hinduism, which at that time was much concerned with making offerings and engaging in rituals. The Buddha's teaching deliberately turned away from those classically religious ways of handling problems, and it is said that the Buddha declined to discuss the question of God as an unhelpful intrusion into considerations of how to deal with the human condition. Because of that, it has sometimes been argued that Buddhism is not so much a religion as a kind of spiritualized humanism, and that seems to be an attractive aspect of Buddhism to many Westerners.

In the Therevada form (now found principally in Sri Lanka and parts of South East Asia), the Buddhism of the monks, or *bhikkhus*, retains a central focus on impermanence. In the Mahayana (chiefly in China, Japan, Korea and Tibet) many schools have developed other kinds of teaching, including Zen, belief in *bodhisattvas* (saviour-like figures who can help others along the path to enlightenment), and worship which includes prayer and obeisance to the Buddhas. But regardless of the school or form of Buddhism, meditation remains central to the practice of most Buddhists.

In all its varied forms, Buddhism has always been a community-centred faith. The role of the *bhikkhus* has been important in providing examples of the living of a spiritual life and of renunciation, and the *sanghas,* or communities of monks, have an important social and cultural, as well as religious role, in Buddhist societies. The relationship between the *sangha* and the surrounding lay society has been one of mutual dependence: the lay people provide the material things needed by the *bhikkhus* – the daily round with bowls to collect food for the day is just one example of that – whilst the *bhikkhus* offer to the laity a model of the Buddhist life which they may not be able to emulate fully but which does keep before them a picture of the life of meditation and compassionate works.

One of the issues for Buddhists in the West is whether and to what extent the traditions need to be re-interpreted in a different cultural and religious context. Should Buddhist monks in the West go out with bowls to solicit food if the surrounding community is not Buddhist? Is it appropriate to wear traditional Asian clothing in Europe? And so on. Not surprisingly, different answers have been given to these questions. Some Buddhist communities have continued to live in close conformity with the traditions of Thailand or Tibet, or wherever the origins of the community may be; others have adopted a distinctly Western style in which to clothe their Buddhist thought and practice.

To some degree those differences were reflected in the early developments of Buddhism in Britain. Philosophers and writers of the nineteenth century (including Schopenhauer and Edwin Arnold) had drawn attention to the attractions of Buddhism. In 1924 the Buddhist Lodge of the Theosophical Society (a Western-founded organization which stimulated interest in Asian religions) became The Buddhist Society of London. That was soon succeeded by The Buddhist Society, which now offers courses in many different kinds of Buddhist teaching, including traditions of the Therevada, and Tibetan and Zen Buddhism. A different kind of development occurred in 1926, when an English convert to Buddhism named *Dharmapala,* who had lived in Sri Lanka and India and had founded the Maha Bodhi Society, established a monastery in the UK for Sinhalese monks. The celebrated Japanese scholar and writer, D. T. Suzuki, visited London in 1936 to attend the World Congress of Faiths, and while in the country lectured widely on Zen.

There have been similar kinds of developments in more recent times. In 1977 an American *bhikkhu* who lived and trained in Thailand established a *sangha* of Western monks in West Sussex (the community is now at Chithurst). Later, branches of the *sangha* established communities in Northumberland, Devon, and Hertfordshire. The work of Japanese *bhikkhus* resulted in the founding of several Japanese Zen societies in Britain. Members of the *Nichiren* sect brought with them their special concern for world peace, and established Peace Pagodas in Milton Keynes (1980) and London (1985). Interest in Tibetan Buddhism has grown considerably in recent years, stimulated by the movement of refugees from Tibet to India, and no doubt by the great respect widely accorded to the Dalai Lama. Many Buddhist communities in Britain today are led by *bhikkhus* who have come from countries in which the various traditions are rooted – Thailand, Japan, the Indian sub-continent, Tibet, Korea. In that way, the traditions are able to feed upon their original sources. A rather different strand of British Buddhism is represented by the Friends of the Western Buddhist Order (FWBO), founded by Sangharakshita, an Englishman who studied Buddhism in India for many years, and was ordained a *bhikkhu* there. The FWBO aims to express the teachings and principles underlying all forms of Buddhism in ways that are particularly accessible to Westerners.

It is difficult to estimate the number of Buddhists in Britain. 'Membership' of Buddhist groups is not necessarily regarded as important in itself; people will come and go, learn meditation and other Buddhist practices, and then practise on their own or in non-Buddhist groups; some will become *bhikkhus* for a limited period, others will make a lifelong commitment. All of this is consistent with Buddhist values and traditions. Estimates of numbers vary widely, suggesting only that in addition to the relatively small number of Asian Buddhists in Britain there are between 10,000 and 100,000 British Buddhists. The Buddhist Directory shows a remarkable spread of Buddhist organizations in the United Kingdom and Ireland, listing over two hundred and forty Buddhist groups, societies, and centres, some twenty temples or pagodas, and several monasteries.[22]

Buddhist ethical teaching emphasizes reverence for life, compassion to all creatures, and the limiting of attachments and possessions. Buddhists are usually vegetarians, and are likely to espouse the values of living simply and limiting the use of non-renewable resources (chapter 12, p. 73). Environmental issues are a natural outlet for Buddhist concern and action, as are policies to do with the pursuit of peace and the abolition of nuclear weapons.

Notes

1. Luke 4.16–30. See Heather A. McKay, 'From Evidence to Edifice: Four Fallacies about the Sabbath' in Robert P. Carroll (ed), *Text as Pretext: Essays in Honour of Robert Davidson, Journal for the Study of the Old Testament*, Supplement Series 138, Sheffield Academic Press 1992.

2. Lionel Blue, *To Heaven with Scribes and Pharisees*, Darton, Longman and Todd 2nd edn 1990, p. 28.

3. Daniele Joly, 'Making a Place for Islam in British Society. Muslims in Birmingham', *Research Papers in Ethnic Relations*, University of Warwick, January 1987, p.1.

4. The Church of England declared in a report: 'We hope that all Christians will be willing to meet with people of other faith communities for the purpose of mutual recognition, friendship and learning. We should not forget that in Britain the Hindu, Muslim and Sikh communities are frequently disadvantaged ethnic minority groups which suffer extensively from racial harassment and social ills such as unemployment and poor housing beyond the average of the white community. They can benefit from Christian acknowledgement and recognition that they exist, that they are devout religious people, and that they are significant parts of the total community. Visiting the temple or the mosque says all that more effectively than words . . .' *'Multi-Faith Worship'?*, published for the General Synod Board of Mission of the Church of England, Church House Publishing 1992, p. 33.

5. Although originally envisaged as multi-faith worship for Commonwealth Day, the strong feelings aroused by that in some Christians has tempered the Abbey's practice, which in most respects is closer to what I have called inter-faith celebration.

6. 'From darkness lead *him* to light, from death lead *him* to eternal life'. Cf. *Brihadaranyaka Upanishad* 1.iii.28: 'From the unreal lead me to the real; from darkness lead me to light; from death lead me to immortality.'

7. C. S. Rodd, *Thinking Things Through* 1. *The Bible*, Epworth Press 1996.

8. Hippolytus, *Expository Treatises Against the Jews*, 7; Chrysostom, *Eight Orations Against the Jews*, 1.7. See Rosemary Ruether, *Faith and Fratricide: The Theological Roots of Anti-Semitism*, Seabury Press, New York 1974, pp. 128–30.

9. Much has been written about these three approaches. Clear discussion about them may be found in, e.g., Alan Race, *Christians and Religious Pluralism*, SCM Press 2nd edn 1993; Gavin D'Costa, *Theology and Religious Pluralism*, Basil Blackwell 1986.

10. See J. A. Dinoia, *The Diversity of Religions*, The Catholic University of America Press, Washington, DC 1992.

11. For a lengthy and very scholarly exposition of this view, see Raimundo Panikkar, *The Silence of God: The Answer of the Buddha*, Orbis, Maryknoll 1990.

12. Wilfred Cantwell Smith, 'The Christian in a Religiously Plural World' in John Hick & Brian Hebblethwaite (eds), *Christianity and Other Religions*, Collins Fount 1980, p. 98.

13. E. F. Schumacher, *Small is Beautiful: A Study of Economics as if People Mattered*, Blond & Briggs 1973, p. 49.

14. William Johnston, *Letters to Contemplatives*, HarperCollins Fount 1991, pp. 24f.; see also Peter D. Bishop, *Clinging to Faith*, Epworth Press 1996, ch. 13.

15. See Masao Abe, in John B. Cobb Jr & Christopher Ives (eds), *The Emptying God: A Buddhist-Jewish-Christian Conversation*, Orbis Books, Maryknoll 1990, p. x: 'I do not mean to say by this that Buddhism and Christianity should aim at a syncretism. Instead, I mean that through such a serious dialogue both Buddhism and Christianity should purify and deepen themselves respectively, and yet, in this way, come to realize a deeper common ground' quoted by Damien Keown, in Cyril S. Rodd (ed), *New Occasions Teach New Duties?*, Epworth Press 1995, p. 204.

16. *Guru Granth Sahib*, 4.1.6, translated by D. A. T. Thomas

17. See Muhammad Anwar, *The Myth of Return. Pakistanis in Britain*, Heinemann 1979.

18. A study conducted by Dr Steven Vertovec, a researcher at Brighton Polytechnic between 1988 and 1992, compared practices at the Vishwa Hindu Kendra and the Sri Ram Mandir in Southall, the Radha-Krishna Temple in Balham and the Caribbean Hindu Society Temple in Brixton. See Steven

Vertovec, 'Community and Congregation in London Hindu Temples: divergent trends', *New Community* 8 (2), pp. 251–264.

19. See A. Helweg, *Sikhs in Britain. The Development of a Migrant Community*, OUP, India, 1979.

20. Parminder Bhachu, *Twice Migrants. East African Sikh Settlers in Britain*, Tavistock Publications 1985, p. 54, wrote of the 'East African' Sikhs: '. . . greater stress has been placed on their "East Africanness" and "Ramgarhianess" which are projected positively in terms of their wealth, education, urban sophistication, and more stringent adherence to Sikhism and ritual proceduures.'

21. Ibid., p. 174.

22. *Buddhist Directory*, Buddhist Society Publications 1997.

Further Reading

Inter-Faith Consultative Group, *'Multi-Faith Worship'?*, Church House Publishing 1992

Deals with issues about sharing in worship and prayer with people of other faiths.

Dan Cohn-Sherbok (ed), *Many Mansions: Inter-Faith and Religious Intolerance*, Bellew Publishing 1992

An uneven collection, but it contains many useful chapters on Christians and other faiths from writers who include George Carey, Robert Runcie, Gavin D'Costa, Alan Race, Michael Nasir-Ali, John Hick and Marcus Braybrooke.

Hans Küng, *Towards a Global Responsibility: In Search of a New World Ethic*, SCM Press 1991
Paul Knitter, *Jesus and Other Names: Christian Mission and Global Responsibility*, Orbis Books, Maryknoll 1996
Alan Race, *Christians and Religious Pluralism*, SCM Press 2nd edn 1993

Important discussions of some of the major issues in inter-faith relations.

M. Braybrooke, *How to Understand Judaism*, SCM Press 1995
Stuart Brown, *The Nearest in Affection: Towards a Christian Understanding of Islam*, WCC Publications 1994
Horst Georg Pöhlmann, *Encounters with Hinduism: A Contribution to Inter-Religious Dialogue*, SCM Press 1996

These three books deal in different ways with actual encounters between Christians and people of three major world faiths.

William Johnston, *Letters to Contemplatives*, HarperCollins Fount 1991

A beautifully written collection of letters to his friends, discussing issues that arise in inter-faith dialogue, from a leading Catholic scholar with an intimate knowledge both of Christian mysticism and of Japanese Buddhism.

W. Owen Cole (ed), *Six World Faiths*, Cassell revised edn 1996

Brief and accessible outlines of Hinduism, Judaism, Buddhism, Christianity, Islam and Sikhism, written by people who profess the faiths they write about.

Roger Hooker & John Sargant (eds), *Belonging to Britain: Christian Perspectives on Religion and Identity in a Plural Society*, CCBI Publications 1991

What does it mean to be a Christian and to be British in a society where Christianity is one belief system alongside many?

Religions in the UK. A Multi-Faith Directory, Religious Resource and Research Centre, University of Derby DE3 5GX

Reprinting in 1997, this is a comprehensive guide to Britain's major religious communities.

Useful Addresses

The Inter Faith Network for the United Kingdom,
5–7 Tavistock Place,
London WC1H 9SN   (Tel. 0171-387-7968)

The Council of Christians and Jews,
Drayton House,
30 Gordon Street,
London WC1H 0AN   (Tel. 0171-388-3322)